Mark Greenfield

FAQ THE
PILOT

The 72 Most Popular Questions
Answered From Inside the Cockpit

check ✓ pilot

First published and printed in July 2022
Copyright © Checkpilot™ Publishing House, Austria

Author: Mark Greenfield

Editing: Laura Amanda Scott
                   Matthew Cash
Proofreading: Nik Hammond
                   William Nuessle

Illustrations: Liana Akobian
                   www.lianaakobian.com

ISBN: 978-3-903355-24-8

CONTENT

PLANNING & ORGANIZATION

THE AIRCRAFT

FLYING & ENTERTAINMENT

NAVIGATION & THE COCKPIT

WEATHER & TURBULENCE

FLIGHT ATTENDANTS & PILOTS

SAFETY & WELLBEING

Preface

You would think that traveling by plane is no longer anything out of the ordinary, literally everyone you know or could meet in the street, in a restaurant or at your place of work has experienced the joy of flying?

It may be surprising, but most people have never flown before. Many still dream of one day seeing the world from a bird's-eye perspective and sharing their own experiences of flying. Even for those who regularly set foot on board a plane, be it for work or simply to explore the world, flying still harbors a wide range of fascinating topics and exciting questions that need answering.

Think of the airport as a kind of small, functional (sometimes dysfunctional) city. This is a place where things are done completely differently than in everyday life. Some experience their arrival at the terminal as the start of a wonderful journey, while for others it is a stressful experience of never-ending hustle and bustle. Traveling by plane evokes wildly varying emotions. For those who enjoy flying, traveling by air is normally a truly pleasant experience. To them, a window seat allows them to view the world from above, a change of scenery from that boring and bland office view, while a cold beverage and a good meal helps them to relax and enjoy themselves. Nowhere else besides space, can one admire cloud formations up so close and personal that you feel that you could touch them, or enjoy such extensive views over entire countries!

However, not all passengers enjoy flying or look forward to take-off. In fact, air travel causes unease for many people. Passengers who are particularly afraid of flying often suffer from the feeling of helplessness while on board. These passengers fear not being in control and find it difficult to trust their safety to a crew that is often out of sight behind a locked cockpit door. However, it is not about having trust and faith in the airline; the take-off and landing is not a matter of luck, but a routine act performed by the flight crew. Knowledge of these processes can help to increase your mental well-being on board, no matter how many times you have sat on a plane.

An aircraft is a meeting place, a place for people to socialize. Flights not only connect people, they also create a sense of togetherness among people from varying backgrounds and cultures. Other passengers savor the solitude as a chance for a time-out, the quiet atmosphere of an aircraft cabin being particularly suited to leaving the hustle and bustle of everyday life behind. For example, picking up that book you've been meaning to read, the one that's been lying on the shelf at home for a long time. The time spent on board can therefore be experienced and enjoyed in complete contrast to your normal everyday life.

Throughout my years as a professional pilot, I have been able to compile the most common and interesting questions that passengers have asked me. Providing answers to these questions has led to the creation of this book being written and sharing these contents with you, in order to give you an insight into the world that we as professionals love and experience on a daily basis. Regardless of whether you are planning a city break, business trip or a holiday, this book is a practical companion for all your travel needs. Turn the pages and you will find interesting chapters, giving you background information and basic knowledge about the aviation industry.

Prepared for your journey? You can now let your adventure begin! For your upcoming flight, please fasten your seatbelts, stow your table and ensure your seat is in the upright position. Ladies and Gentlemen, we are cleared for take-off! I wish you an enjoyable and pleasant stay on board, the opportunity to make memorable moments and above all else, a safe trip.

Always happy landings,
Mark Greenfield

At the Airport

Airport codes

When traveling by air, you may have wondered about the airport codes that make no sense whatsoever. Every airport has its own individual, internationally recognized code. It is used to ensure that all passengers and their baggage arrive at the correct destination.

For airline passengers, these so-called »3-letter codes« are visible identifiers of their departure and arrival airports. Made up of three Latin letters, these codes are assigned to all airports by the *International Air Transport Association* (IATA), the umbrella organization for all airlines.

Whenever possible, it uses the first letters of the respective city's English spelling. Hence, *Miami* airport in the USA is abbreviated to »MIA«, Germany's *Frankfurt* airport to »FRA«, the city state of *Singapore* to »SIN«, *Sydney* in Australia to »SYD« and *Cairo* in Egypt to »CAI«.

When an abbreviation has already been used, sometimes entirely random codes are assigned. Firstly, however, there is an attempt to use individual letters found in the destination's name.
Examples include the airport code of »JNB« for *Johannesburg* in South Africa, »SFO« for *San Francisco* in the USA and »BKK« for *Bangkok* airport in Thailand.

Cities with more than one airport may receive »3-letter codes« based upon regional reference points or they may include the initials of famous celebrities. This is how the thirty-fifth president of the United States, John F. Kennedy, came to lend his name to one of New York City's airports and its code of »JFK«. In France, one of the three Parisian airports is named after the former French statesman Charles de Gaulle, hence its code »CDG«.

As well as »3-letter codes«, the aviation industry further designates »4-letter codes«. These are assigned by the *International Civil Aviation Organization* (ICAO) and are essential for the worldwide connectivity of air traffic.

When flying from Rome to Stockholm, for example, the flight crew will program the route using the codes »LIRF« to »ESSA«. Here, the first letter indicates the continent or region. Southern European nations such as Italy receive the code »L«, while Northern European countries are assigned the letter »E«. Based on the same principle, »R« stands for countries in East Asia, »K« for the USA and »S« for nations in South America.

The second letter refers directly to the countries of departure and arrival. Thus, »I« in our example stands for Italy and »S« for Sweden. The third and fourth letters are used to give every airport its individual identification marker. »RF« stands for Rome's main airport of Fiumicino and »SA« for Stockholm's Arlanda Airport.

Aviation authorities, air traffic control, aviation weather services, manufacturing, and maintenance companies as well as airlines operate with these combinations. These internationally valid codes have thus been established to prevent confusion. For you, the travelling passenger, looking at your luggage tag, the »3-letter code« will suffice.

How to identify airplane types

Passenger planes used for charter and scheduled flights are made by a relatively small number of manufacturers. These manufacturers produce a wide variety of different models, however. The most famous manufacturers, some of which you will be familiar with, include Airbus, Boeing, Bombardier and Embraer. Some you may be less familiar with include Ilyushin, Sukhoi and Tupolev.

At first glance, it is not easy to distinguish one model from another, as the basic shape of most airplanes is very similar. The distinction often comes down to details. Features such as the length of the fuselage, or the number of- or position of the engines. The number of wheels or shape of the wings allow the differences to be more easily identified.

For example, when directly comparing two of the most common short or medium-range jets, the »Airbus A320« has a more rounded nose than the »Boeing 737« whose nose is distinctly more pointed. The Airbus, it is believed, has a happy face, while the Boeing's face looks more stern. You can be the judge of that.

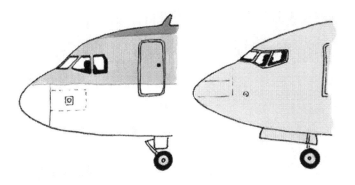

Besides external features, aircraft are categorized as short, medium or long-haul models. However, there is no internationally recognized definition of these individual ranges, which is why authorities, aircraft manufacturers and airlines often define them quite differently.

Inside the plane, the seat arrangements are chosen exclusively by the individual airline. This is why it is difficult and almost impossible to distinguish aircraft types based upon the design or the features of an interior. Long-haul aircraft certainly don't make that any easier as they offer a multitude of seat arrangement options.

A simple trick may help you have an idea as to what type or variation of aircraft you are on: most airlines advertise a small string of letters on the fuselage, normally located by the rear exit. This allows you to identify the type of aircraft. If you missed that, simply have a look at the *safety card* in the seat pocket in front of you. It will tell you what type of plane you have just boarded.

Aircraft registration

Similar to cars, aircraft are assigned to their respective owners by means of an individual registration. This registration number must be clearly visible on the rear part of the fuselage, sometimes in combination with a national or union flag (for instance the European Union flag). On commercial planes, the precise nationality and identification are established by a series of letters and numbers.

Country codes derived from the name of the respective nation are a bit easier to recognize. »C« is for *Canada*, for instance. A plane registered in *Italy* is given the country code »I«. In *France*, an aircraft's nationality is indicated by the letter »F«.

Other registrations seem strange at first glance. The Netherlands, for example, use »PH« as their country code, and the USA uses the designator »N«. For example, at a convention in Paris on 13 October 1919 it was decided that the Netherlands would take the national letter H and the US would be given N and W, followed by four letters. However as there were more countries starting with an H, such as Haiti and Hungary, it was changed to H-N followed by three letters. The choice was not universally popular. The Journal Aviation wanted the U.S. to adopt W in honor of the Wright brothers. Following the International Radiotelegraph Conference in Washington in 1927, the Dutch registration was changed to »PH«.

What comes after the first letter is exclusively determined by national regulations. Many countries try to apply a system that is plausible to them. Austrian planes use the country code »OE«, for example. The following letter specifies the plane's weight class. »A« stands for a single-engine plane with a maximum weight of 4,400 pounds (2,000 kilograms). Sports aircraft are in this category. Commercial aircraft with a permissible total weight of more than 44,000 pounds (20,000 kilograms) are labeled with an »L«. Among others, this category includes the »Boeing 777-200«.

Security checks – a stress factor

All airports consist of two areas: *landside* and *airside*. The landside is normally open to the public, even without a ticket. You can say goodbye to your loved ones, a colleague or family member and welcome them back there. Those in possession of a valid ticket are allowed into the airside area of the airport. After passing a security check you enter airside, where you will find infinite possibilities to eat, drink or purchase gifts. It is also where you will find and be provided access to your gate.

One of the many tasks assigned to the security staff is to prevent unauthorized access to the airside portion of the airport. Access is only granted to passengers with valid travel documents and flight tickets via a security check. These checks also apply to cleaning staff, delivery services, airport and airline personnel.

Every single person is required to carry a special photo ID containing a magnetic strip coded with their respective access rights. The ID's color indicates their accessible work area. The majority of airports use gray, green, blue, yellow and red. Gray representing the lowest level of access authorization and red the highest.

All persons working airside at the airport, whether they be fueling the plane, loading baggage or maintenance engineers as well as flight and cabin crew, will be assigned a red ID. In order to receive this level of access they are required to complete regular training and exams. As well as have a comprehensive and criminal background check. The focus of these exams is for each person to be proficient in the latest regulatory, security and precautionary measures.

The security personnel's second largest area of responsibility is to check hand luggage for prohibited items. Items such as weapons, narcotics, explosives and incendiaries are generally prohibited without predetermined special authorization. Post 911, these items are deemed to be capable of endangering aircraft safety or immobilizing a member of airport or airline staff.

Airport staff are known to be extremely strict when it comes to implementing these regulations. Items packed by mistake must be removed from your hand luggage and are disposed of by the security staff. If you don't want to lose it, don't pack it in your hand luggage! Due to their sharp surfaces, everyday items such as razors, nail files and scissors must be stored in your checked-in suitcase. Items such as additional clothing, baby bottles, baby food, photo and video cameras, contact lens cleaning fluid and medication in solid or liquid form can be carried in hand luggage.

These organized checks are designed to prevent hijackings, terror attacks or sabotage. They regularly cause confusion and anger, with passengers questioning to what extent they are appropriate. Long queues further test passenger patience, especially when they are already in a hurry to catch their flight.

Visual inspections of travel bags and hand luggage are perceived as particularly unpleasant. However, they are necessary when prohibited items are identified during an x-ray check or if potential dangers cannot be judged reliably based on the scanned information. Even if some of the items in your hand luggage you may not want a stranger to see, you can rest assured, airport security staff have already seen it all and handle such situations very professionally.

Finally, metal detectors are a major source of stress too. Those who carry metal objects on their person and forget to put them on the x-ray belt are sure to attract the attention of security staff. Many passengers dread this unpleasant beep of the metal detector, which may result in uncomfortable questions. Especially in countries where passengers do not speak the language, they are often afraid of having to explain things.

However, not every alarm is »real«. Sometimes a random generator triggers an alarm when a passenger steps through the metal detector gate, regardless of whether the passenger is actually carrying metal items or not. This is intentional. The alarm is designed to go off regularly to signal to the passengers waiting in line: »No one gets through here with prohibited items – we will find everything – we are on to you!«

The alarm itself is not even a decisive factor for security staff. They pay greater attention to the display behind the metal detector which shows, on a tiered scale, the number of metal items a passenger is carrying. A cell phone in one's pocket triggers an alarm level similar to that caused by a prohibited weapon. This is why emptying your pockets beforehand and placing metal items on the belt not only speeds up the whole process but is also easier on your nerves – and those of the security staff.

Security measures of course differ from airport to airport and country to country. This is due to the fact that the International Civil Aviation Organization ICAO only recommends minimum standards for the implementation of security regulations to its member states. Based on those, every country is free to implement its own suitable measures to maintain general safety.

It goes without saying that security measures are stepped up in the event of an acute threat or routes to riskier areas of the world. One example of a more intensive process is to fly to the Israeli airport of Tel Aviv. Ben Gurion is the epitome of security. All arriving private cars, taxis, and trucks pass a security checkpoint even before reaching the airport terminal. This is followed by a detailed series of checks that continue right up until boarding commences. A practical tip: when flying to or departing from Israel, allow plenty of time, at least three hours prior to your scheduled departure time.

Metal detectors vs. body scanners

Personal property is to be deposited before the security screening. This includes coats, sweaters, necklaces and the entire contents of pants pockets. To avoid unpleasant surprises, it is advisable to familiarize yourself with prohibited items before embarking on a journey.

You will be asked to place hand luggage and all items carried with you in the trays provided, after which they are conveyed through an x-ray device and meticulously examined. Security staff are able to spot prohibited items at a glance and if they do, the passenger is obliged to open their bags and dispose of the respective items. In the event that staff are unsure whether a prohibited item is contained in the luggage, a manual follow-up inspection follows. Sometimes, staff completely empty bags to make sure nothing is overlooked.

In the meantime, passengers must step through the metal detector. Certain airports additionally require them to take off belts and shoes. With cold feet and your pants hanging down, you then step through the metal detector gate.

Stepping through creates a weak, low-frequency magnetic field. It recognizes metal, allowing the detection of weapons or other potentially dangerous items. If it detects a sufficient amount of metal, it emits an acoustic signal.

The gate's sensitivity is individually adjusted by the respective airport. The more sensitive the device is, the smaller the amounts of metal needed to trigger a signal. This is the reason that even rings, piercings, clothing inserts – for example in bras – and even prostheses can trigger a signal.

If you have a knee or hip replacement or a pacemaker, it is recommended to carry your implant ID with you for every flight. These devices do not react to dental implants, on the other hand. The amount of metal in those is too small to be recognized by the detector.

Apart from the usual metal detector gates, some airports choose to work with body scanners. These so-called »passive« scanners detect the human body's radiation and use it to find items worn on the body.

Only »active« body scanners use weak x-rays to detect metal. These rays' higher frequencies allows for better image resolution and therefore more reliable detection of prohibited weapons. However, the use of these scanners is controversial in many countries, which is why they are seldom used at airports.

Barcodes on travel bags

To make sure your check-in baggage finds its way to your destination without getting lost, it is fitted with a white paper loop with an individual barcode printed on it. This so-called »baggage tag« is a luggage sticker made of a tear-proof material that contains data about its owner.

Apart from the departure and arrival airport, it provides information on any booked transfers. Both the international abbreviation of the airline and the current flight number are shown on the tag, along with the passenger's full name and gender. Also included is the code for the particular check-in counter, or where the »baggage tag« was printed. When scanned, it also reads the date of issue and boarding number. The latter shows your position in the order of passengers checking in. All this information is coded into your individual barcode and printed onto the paper tag both horizontally and vertically. Due to these two different barcode positions, the various automatic baggage conveying system scanners are able to record the necessary data quickly and easily. Every paper tag has an individual number and can thus be clearly allocated.

Special rules apply to travel within the European Union (EU) due to its free movement of goods. Check-in baggage is labeled with a green stripe at the edge of the tag. This enables customs to determine at a glance which suitcases and bags are coming from a country outside of the EU and might therefore need to be checked in more detail.

To allow you to prove that your travel bag belongs to you in case of doubt, you receive a tear-off stub that contains exactly the same information as your »baggage tag«. Once you have arrived at your destination, it serves as a piece of identification when retrieving your luggage at the carousel. In rare cases, airport staff will ask you to produce this stub on request. It also makes it much easier to find lost baggage.

Furthermore, it is important to never remove this stub before the customs check, as it makes it impossible to allocate baggage clearly to passengers and unnecessarily complicates checks.

To prevent theft, you should never entrust a stranger with your personal belongings. Leaving baggage unattended, as well as removing someone else's travel bag from the carousel consciously and intentionally, may result in a fine or air travel ban. To prevent mix-ups, it is a good idea to quickly check your own barcode. After all, other passengers might own a suitcase that matches yours in type and color!

Despite its sturdy material, the paper tag can become damaged or lost at any time. Personalized baggage tags provide additional protection against mix-ups. Ideally, they should contain your contact data and full name in legible writing. Your exact (residential) address should only be indicated inside your suitcase to avoid giving away details of a potentially empty home.

Your luggage on tour

There is a lot to bear in mind from choosing your bag at home to taking it off the carousel at your arrival airport. First, you need to check the maximum size and weight restrictions the respective airline imposes on check-in baggage. As there are no uniform international standards for these, they not only differ from airline to airline but also within certain route networks and according to the booked seat category. Weighing your suitcase before leaving home can prevent unpleasant surprises at the airport. Exceeding the specified maximum weight usually results in surcharges.

Immigration and import regulations determine what items can be taken on board. They can be found on the Internet for every country. Once packed, your travel bag should be easy to close to prevent the closure from becoming damaged. Prior to embarking, take a picture of the contents and the suitcase's exterior to be able to prove possible damage or loss later on. Important travel documents, essential medication, keys and other items of special value should be carried in your hand luggage.

If possible, make sure no belts, straps and loops protrude from your suitcase. These can easily result in damage to your own and other people's luggage. Old barcode tags from previous journeys should be removed before embarking on another trip, as this could lead to confusion in the computer-controlled baggage conveying systems. Suitcases the system was not able to record are subject to manual checks which requires additional time. In the worst case, your baggage misses your flight.

Fragile items should be carefully packed and protected. After all, once your suitcase is put on the conveyor belt at the check-in, it is in for a fast and bumpy ride. These conveyor belts reach an average speed of 5 miles per hour (or 8 kilometers per hour) which, if needed, can be doubled on newer systems. Thousands of pieces of luggage are thus processed, sorted and transported to the x-ray check every hour!

If an alarm is triggered, specially trained airport personnel take a closer look. In case of doubt, the suitcase is opened. A notification later provides information on the reason for the inspection and what items – if any – were removed. If there is nothing to report or check, your luggage continues its journey to the loading station. In case your flight is delayed, or you have booked special service offers such as day-before check-in, your luggage is deposited in a designated storage area. In time for take-off, baggage staff collect it and transport it directly to the plane.

Depending on the loading method and aircraft size, the loading process takes on average around thirty minutes. Baggage is usually stored in containers which are then lifted into the aircraft's fuselage. On other types of planes, suitcases and bags are loosely stored in a baggage compartment. This compartment is then secured with nets and straps. It is a tough job for loading staff, as even heavy baggage is unloaded by hand at the arrival airport before you can retrieve it from the carousels at the arrival terminal.

Family & Pets

How to travel with your children and NOT lose your mind

Flights with children can be significantly more stressful for the parents than it is for their offspring. The unease parents experience under pressure is often subconsciously transferred onto their kids. It is no wonder then that all those involved can quickly reach their stress limits. And all that despite the fact that additional strain on the nerves can be avoided with good preparation, making sure that all family members can embark on their journey in a relaxed manner.

Creating checklists is a good way to keep on top of things. These can take the form of packing and shopping lists or good old-fashioned to-do lists. You have to find out for yourself what kind of list works best for you. A time schedule listing everything to be done by the day of departure and the approximate time each one will take also helps. This allows you to see at a glance what needs to be done when and avoids time pressure.

As the day often does not go to plan with children, it is a good idea to be as prepared as possible. For example, you should buy public transport tickets in advance to avoid the stress of having to queue for longer than expected in front of a counter. Even information on parking at the airport can be researched in advance to avoid annoying parking space scrambles. The more time you allow for your arrival at the airport, the greater the chance of reaching the terminal without time pressure.

Upon arrival, you should check in quickly to get rid of your heavy suitcases and secure convenient seats, if these were not already reserved at the time of booking. Online check-in systems are often available that further reduce stress on the day of departure. Some airlines even make it possible to order children's menus in advance to make sure your little ones are well taken care of on board. After all, a full child is happier than a hungry one. However, you should be careful when it comes to foods with a high sugar content. Due to their stimulating effect, such food items should be avoided both before and during a flight.

Bridging the long wait between check-in and boarding is often a challenge. Most departure terminals offer little distraction for kids and quickly induce boredom. In any case, children should be allowed to move around and let off steam before the flight instead of just sitting around on an airport bench. They will have to sit still for a long time soon enough on the flight.

To make long walking distances more enjoyable, some airports offer a stroller hire service. However, your own folding stroller can also be taken along in the plane. Airlines offer this as family-friendly additional service and do not charge extra for it. Many airports allow you to use strollers right up to the aircraft door. And even if the airline staff do not offer it to you at the gate anyway, the other passengers will surely understand that parents with a stroller should enter the aircraft first. A little head start like this will help you store your items in peace.

All activities and your time on board should be as pleasant as possible. Children especially should wear comfortable clothes during the flight. Depending on the kids' age, their parents' hand luggage should furthermore contain small snacks and entertainment such as favorite toys or a book.

In any case, pack a warm change of clothes, as the aircraft's air conditioning system can make the cabin rather chilly, especially on long flights. If you embark on your flight during the night, routine rituals such as putting on pajamas can serve as a prompt that it is bedtime. A cuddly toy can also help your little ones fall asleep. Unfortunately, these tricks do not work on all kids. As their parents, you will know best how to entertain them.

Extended play time with electronic devices is not recommended as a means of passing the time on board. Some parents use this as a kind of reward which can have the unwanted effect that it is tempting for children to stay up longer to play. Digital distractions disturb children's natural sleep cycle and lead to a lack of sleep.

If your offspring is anxious about flying, it is important to create positive associations. Addressing the topic of flying in a playful way can help. Model airplanes given to the child weeks in advance can serve as a means of explanation prior to departure. At the same time, they can be used as a lucky charm, even though the focus should be on fun. In any case, you should take your child's concerns seriously and be as supportive as you can on the day of the flight. Perhaps a model airplane will even induce a sense of anticipation and help put a smile on your kid's face.

Babies in the air

Of course, every child is unique and behaves differently. Nevertheless, you should refrain from unnecessary air travel during the first few days after giving birth. After that, your child's flight tolerance depends on its health. Some airlines allow you to take babies on board that are just a few days old. Others specify a higher minimum age in their general terms and conditions of carriage for passengers.

Many fellow travelers are concerned that babies will constantly cry in the aircraft cabin, creating an unpleasant atmosphere.

Even parents themselves usually hope to be spared this test of patience. However, experience shows that this concern is often unfounded. Most babies make quiet and courageous passengers. Usually they surprise even their own parents – not to mention all other passengers – by spending the entire flight, or at least the majority of it, fast asleep, arriving well and relaxed.

Expecting mothers should bear in mind the following: during a normal pregnancy, air travel should not be a problem for the health of the unborn child. In accordance with this, most airlines allow flights up to the 35th week of pregnancy. After that, the risk of suddenly going into labor or spontaneous delivery is too high for the airlines, which is why they advise against flying or will even refuse you. In case of high-risk pregnancies or signs of complications, you should refrain from flying entirely.

Let's talk about the youngest passengers on board

Babies and infants under the age of two are regarded as the youngest passengers on board. Up to this age, they are allowed to be seated on their parents' laps. When forgoing their own seat, airlines usually charge a low or no fee at all for carrying infants. However, having a child sitting on your lap will become increasingly uncomfortable as the flight progresses. Be aware before embarking that this cumbersome position can induce stress and irritability and thus stand in the way of a relaxed trip.

Those between two and twelve are classified as children. The authorities require parents of children in this group to book a designated seat for them to ensure adequate safety during take-off and landing and when experiencing turbulence. Many airlines offer price reductions in the form of children's fares, however. Children are only allowed to travel accompanied and are required to carry their own passport. More and more parents live or work in far-away places. Sometimes, it is simply impossible for them to accompany their offspring. This is why children – usually from the age of five – are also allowed to travel as unaccompanied minors. On such a flight, the airline assumes the responsibility for the child through designated minding services at the airport as well as the crew on board.

Airlines that offer this service for unaccompanied minors usually charge additional fees. If this type of childminding works for you, you should gather as much information on the special conditions of this service as you can in advance. Children themselves usually get used to this new experience quickly – not least because they get lots of attention from their individual escort. However, it is not recommended to have a child embark on their very first flight alone. With all the impressions they will gather, parents and other familiar people can give the child an important feeling of safety and answer any questions in a way that they can understand.

Can air travel be fun for seniors?

Many elderly people like traveling just as much as younger generations. However, priorities and personal care needs change over the years. Experienced air travel passengers develop strategies to maintain their well-being, but even they may also require comprehensive support.

Resorting to other people for help is often not an easy thing to do, but if it is necessary then airport staff are at the ready around the clock. It is helpful to seek information in advance about where to go to receive the necessary help. It would be a pity if you had to cancel your journey because of a lack of knowledge or embarrassment. Most concerns can be alleviated by thorough preparation, after all.

It is recommended to arrive at the airport early to avoid time pressure. Be aware that you might have to walk long and tiring distances. To help passengers with reduced mobility, airports provide appropriate walking aids that you can borrow. Access to aircraft is also barrier-free, which means that a wheelchair service is available from the check-in counter directly to the gate at no charge, if needed. If you require an even higher level of support, this service is even extended all the way into the cabin.

A practical tip: If older passengers use an airport golf cart assistance, their travelling partner or companion should also use this service, even if they do not have mobility problems. Getting to gate 138 can be very tiring, especially if you have to dog trot alongside a golf cart.

Many airports have better first-aid equipment than other public buildings. During operating hours, trained, sometimes even medically qualified personnel are available to provide quick support. To be optimally prepared, you should adapt your travel pharmacy to your respective plans and destination and keep it in your carry-on baggage, so it is always within reach. This ensures that you always have required medication at the ready, even if your checked-in luggage is delayed.

Lack of movement, a cramped seat and drinking insufficient water increase the chance of suffering from travel thrombosis and can make your legs swell. Wearing compression stockings helps to prevent possible blood stasis. Medical self-treatment, for example administering a thrombosis injection, should take place prior to embarking. For individual recommendations, consult a physician in advance.

Elderly air travelers should furthermore carefully consider their choice of destination, for not every country is suitable as a vacation region. Climatic changes and acclimatizing to different time zones can take an additional toll on the body. Although this is a factor that applies regardless of one's age, the body needs more time to adapt with advancing age, so that the first days of vacation may be less restful than you would hope.

In order to provide financial incentives for air travel, some airlines offer reduced fares for elderly people. When booking, it is advisable to choose a row of seats in the immediate vicinity of the lavatories and reserving an aisle seat allows you to get up unhindered. Sometimes, you can pay a surcharge to be allowed to board before the other passengers. Such little additional services can increase your travel comfort and happiness.

Four-legged passengers

Most pet owners treat their fur babies like treasured members of their family. As faithful friends and providers of emotional support, they are an important part of a person's life. In light of this, it is little wonder that travelers do not want to exclude their beloved animals from traveling with them.

Still, you should first ask yourself whether it is necessary to take your little furry friend with you on a plane journey. During transport, animals are subjected to countless environmental factors. These include high noise levels, significant temperature fluctuations, changes in air pressure, lack of movement, long waiting times and unfamiliar surroundings – and they have to cope with all of that without their owner by their side. These factors cause considerable stress to animals, which is why you should carefully consider beforehand how much sense it makes to take them along.

Once you have decided to do so, you should start to make a thorough plan early on. Above all, you should familiarize yourself with the import and export regulations of your destination, possible vaccination and quarantine rules, as well as local animal protection standards. All of these usually differ from those in your home country. Correctly completed customs papers and documents sometimes require days or weeks of preparation, so ensure you think ahead!

There is another reason why it is recommended to buy your ticket in good time before the planned departure date: many airlines limit the number of animals carried along on each flight and booking early increases your chances of securing a place.

Generally, every airline is free to decide whether it wants to transport pets at all; not every carrier offers this option. This also applies when traveling with a service or emotional support animal under U.S. law. If it is possible to take the animal into the cabin, most airlines limit this option to cats and small dogs carried in a transport box. The animals' size and weight are strictly specified. Larger dogs and other pets can embark on their journey in the air-conditioned cargo hold. Transport containers for this type of transportation are subject to much more extensive rules.

To provide further care, larger airports often run animal care stations with trained personnel. Before the animals are loaded, specialists check their travel fitness one last time. If the option is available, direct flights should always be preferred. In case this is not possible, the animals receive water and food during stopovers.

Even if your intentions are good, administering tranquilizers and sedatives is considered controversial because of possible side effects. Instead of medication, specialists of veterinary medicine recommend lots of exercise before putting the animals in their transport box. Subject to prior booking, animals that cannot be transported in a passenger aircraft, such as horses, can be carried safely by animal transport services. A cargo airline will then handle the actual transport.

Aircraft Cabin & Health

Searching for row 13

It is recommended to choose your seat as early as possible to get the one you want and to avoid sitting separately from your family or friends. Vigilant passengers may have noticed that the seat row numbering in aircraft operated by certain airlines is incomplete. Omitting the numbers 13 and 17 is particularly common; certain Asian airlines are also missing a row 4. In some cultures, these are considered unlucky numbers. To avoid putting off any passengers, the airlines simply skip the respective numbers.

In aircraft cabins, rows of seats are numbered in sequence from the front to the back. Looking towards the cockpit, window row »A« is located on the left. Center seats are labeled »B« while aisle seats are indicated by the letter »C«. If another row of three seats is located on the opposite side, the letters follow the alphabet: »D« indicating the aisle seat, »E« the middle one and »F« the window seat. If the seat diagram does not include the letters »B« or »E«, there is no center seat. This indicates that the plane is equipped with a row of two seats.

Long-haul aircraft offer space for a third row of seats. On planes with a three-four-three configuration, the letter »I« is swapped for the letter »J«. Airlines do this to avoid possible confusion with the number 1 when passengers look for their seats.

What makes a »perfect« seat, however, is in the eye of the beholder alone. Neither numbers nor letters stand for the general quality of an individual seat. If you book early, you can reserve the seat of your choice. For this purpose, some airlines publish seat arrangement diagrams for their aircraft.

Mobile devices and cell phones

When mobile devices became items of everyday use many years ago, there were concerns that cell phone frequencies might interfere with radio communication and ground station signals (for example navigation systems). Research has shown that those concerns are unfounded. They can, however, impede radio communication between the pilot and air traffic controllers, since devices capable of transmitting such as cell phones constantly search for a signal. In practice, this most likely applies to aircraft where the distance between the cockpit and the rows of seats behind is particularly small.

Telephone use is prohibited in modern passenger aircraft for both comfort and safety reasons, as well as to not bother fellow passengers. Even if only every second person took out their cell phone and started making a call, the result would be chatter of »Babylonian« dimensions, bearing a great potential for conflict. In polls carried out so far, the majority of air travelers have rejected the idea of allowing phone calls on board.

Additionally, such regulations prevent passengers from getting distracted by their own devices, encouraging them to pay more active attention to the crew's announcements. This can be vital, especially in the event of an emergency. Nevertheless, the use of cell phones is permitted during take-off and landing, provided their transmitting functions are deactivated.

Myths related to aircraft doors

The thought that someone could open an aircraft door in the air causes unease among most people, evoking concerns of passengers being sucked out of the aircraft during the flight. However, this fantastical notion is largely fueled by the film industry. What may be feasible on a film set, however, is in fact impossible in reality.

Before leaving the gate, all exits are locked by the cabin crew and double-checked from the cockpit via electric signals. Once the plane is in the air, the heavy cabin doors are pressed into their mounts by the air flow. A pressure of more than one ton is then applied to every single exit. It is therefore entirely impossible to open such a door by simply pushing against it with one's body weight.

That little hole in the window

Aircraft windows differ from those in your home in many ways. The manufacturing processes involved are technically much more elaborate as they need to withstand much greater loads.

The most obvious difference lies in their typical oval shape which serves purposes of safety. Constant pressure changes put aircraft windows under a lot of stress, which could cause hairline cracks at the edges of rectangular windows. With an oval design, the pressure applied is more evenly distributed, which avoids this problem.

However, the structure of the overall design is much more complex than one might think. Every passenger window consists in detail of three individual panes: one sturdy outer pane and two inner safety panes. Passengers with a window seat may have noticed the little hole in the lower area of the middle and inner pane?

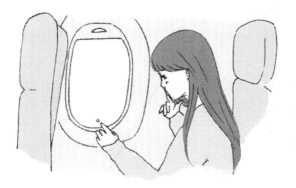

It may be the cause of some concern at first glance, but in fact it is of essential importance. This small hole serves pressure equalization purposes and prevents possible damage due to constant pressure changes. Furthermore, it vents the cavity between the individual glass panes, preventing insufficient air circulation in this area which could lead to condensation. This would result in fogged-up windows, robbing window seat passengers of many amazing views.

Not only is the shape carefully chosen, the window size is also a decisive factor in aircraft construction. Airplanes are supposed to deal with high summer temperatures on the ground just as well as with ice-cold outside temperatures at cruising altitude. Their materials constantly expand and contract. Even one unsealed spot in the window could turn into a serious problem. The solution lies in the size of the glass panes: the smaller the window, the lower the risk of an unwanted gap between the frame and the glass.

Some aircraft such as the »Boeing 787« feature a new design that replaces the familiar manually adjustable sunshades. Between two of the flat glass panes there is a wafer-thin layer of conductive gel which changes its color due to electrical stimulation, dimming the window in the process. If no electrical energy is applied, the window remains transparent. These modern aircraft windows were designed in such a way that they dim automatically according to outside light conditions. However, passengers are still able to control them individually.

Ashtrays in the lavatory

Today, there are almost no airlines that permit smoking on board. Giving in to this craving is made impossible at every opportunity in modern planes. Loudspeaker announcements and a crossed-out cigarette icon above the seats draw attention to this strict ban. Passengers are even reminded of it in the lavatories. It is therefore all the more surprising that, of all places in an aircraft, it is equipped with an ashtray.

There is a simple and obvious reason for that: despite smoking on board being strictly banned and dangerous, not all passengers comply with this rule. The ashtray in the lavatory is therefore simply a precautionary measure. If a smoker decides to ignore all warnings, it allows them to properly dispose of their lit cigarettes. Tobacco products carelessly thrown into garbage bins can seriously compromise the safety of all people on board. Paper towels and other disposed items are easily flammable which could result in a fire quickly spreading to other areas of the cabin.

To reduce the risk of a fire, every lavatory is equipped with a sensitive smoke detector. If the alarm is triggered, a loud signal is emitted in both the cockpit and the entire cabin. The flight crew, prepared by regular training, will investigate the alarm immediately, because in the worst case there is little time to get the flames under control.

Since smoking on board not only represents a violation of rules but also the endangerment of human lives, flight bans, high fines and even prison sentences are imposed in individual cases. It is therefore advisable to think of an individual strategy for how to get through a potentially long flight without puffing on a cigarette.

Is toilet waste dumped in the air?

There are different toilet systems, two of which have established themselves in the aviation industry. On-board toilets are closed-loop systems, meaning that their contents are not dumped during the flight but instead routed into a storage tank underneath the lavatory cabin. Only once the plane has touched down are the contents then emptied by a special vehicle. This process only takes a few minutes, after which the lavatory is ready for use once more.

Business jets often use water-flush systems, which work rather like camping toilets. Since a continuous freshwater supply is simply impossible on an airplane, between four and ten liters of water (depending on the system) are constantly circulated through the flush system and are available for repeated use. The liquid's blue hue is due to the chemical additives required to assure the necessary hygiene. They delay the natural decay processes to allow the next person to use the toilet without being subjected to foul odors.

The water-flush system is not suitable for large passenger aircraft, however. The volumes of water required would simply weigh too much. To make sure a fully booked passenger plane can still provide functional toilets for many hours, excrements are routed into a collection tank by means of negative pressure. The pressure difference between the cabin and outside the aircraft makes this possible. When flushing the toilet, the collecting tank's flap opens with a bang and your business is literally sucked away. This suction effect is so strong that it reliably prevents blockages. Small amounts of liquid are optional added to the process to remove residue sticking to the bowl. So where does the widespread belief that toilet waste is dumped in the air come from?

In fact, rare cases of »blue ice« falling from the sky have been sighted in the vicinity of airports. This phenomenon occurs when the collecting tank's seals become brittle or the drain valve has not been closed properly. Small drops of water can thus reach the aircraft's outer shell. They freeze at exit and slowly thaw as the plane enters warmer atmospheric layers during descent. At some point, they detach and fall down. »Blue ice« dropping from the sky may be a spectacular sight, but such occurrences are extremely rare. Thorough maintenance and properly functioning exterior valves prevent possible damage on the ground and provide maximum safety.

Why is the cabin pressurized?

A passenger plane's average cruising altitude is approximately *36,000 feet (11,000 meters)*. At this altitude, humans are incapable of breathing naturally without technical help. This is why the cabin is constantly pressurized to roughly *8,000 feet (2,500 meters)* above sea level during the flight. This allows all passengers to breathe without difficulty.

Extreme mountaineers know that the so-called »death zone«, in which the human body requires an additional oxygen supply, starts at about *23,000 feet (7,000 meters)*. The oxygen saturation in the blood decreases continuously with altitude. The result is a deficiency of oxygen in the tissue also referred to as hypoxia. To allow us to breathe and travel without harmful consequences in an aircraft, artificial pressure has to be built up in the cabin. On modern commercial planes, the optimum air pressure is controlled automatically. The plane's engines drive a compressor that compresses the intake air. Far too hot at this point, some of this compressed air is transported to a cooling unit and fed into the air conditioning system from there. Now the fresh air can be mixed with the cabin air and ensure a pleasant climate on board.

In the event that the automatic pressure regulation system ceases to work, the pressure can also be controlled manually from the cockpit. In exceptionally rare cases of total failure, oxygen masks are located in a compartment above the seat. To make sure children sitting on their parents' laps and flight crew working in the aisles can be supplied with oxygen immediately, there are always more masks than seats. If needed, they fall from the ceiling and supply passengers in a fully booked plane with air to breathe for about fifteen to twenty minutes. This is enough time to descend to an altitude where breathing is possible without a mask. After that, the pilot will land the plane at the nearest airport.

Why does flying makes you gassy?

Does this question seem inappropriate to you? In fact, questions about annoying digestion problems are asked very often, unofficially and in strict confidence, of course. But it is easy to explain why your digestive system makes itself known with particular vigor high up in the air.

Changing cabin pressure has an effect on your body: if it increases, it does not take long for residual gas to be forced out, causing flatulence. For many air travelers this turns into a true nightmare – who wants to create a literally »bad atmosphere« between oneself and one's fellow passengers, after all?

However, a few simple tricks can help reduce or even prevent the effects of annoying digestive issues: avoid eating gas-inducing food such as legumes or cabbage before embarking on airplane travel. Make sure to drink plenty of still water. Carbonated beverages and alcohol, on the other hand, tend to have the opposite effect. On longer flights, it can help to wear comfortable clothing and refrain from using a tight belt, to prevent further compressing your abdomen. Short walks up and down the aisle can also help your body get rid of gases.

Flying with a cold

A cold affects your inner ear, which is responsible for modulating pressure. Changing cabin pressure during climb and descent require pressure equalization in the inner ear. This is not a problem for healthy individuals, as an aircraft's pressurized cabin supports the natural process of gradual pressure adaptation. When suffering from a cold, however, the body loses this capability. If you still decide to fly off to your vacation with a flu-like infection and clogged sinuses, you risk suffering permanent damage.

The human ear is designed in such a way that the middle ear starts right behind the eardrum. Located there, next to the ossicles, is an important cavity that is filled with air and cushioned by mucous membranes. This small cavity is connected to the mouth and throat region by the Eustachian tube and ensures internal venting and pressure modulation. When suffering from colds and infections, however, this tube gets blocked. Due to the now lower internal pressure, the ear drum is sucked into the middle ear when landing, which can result in pain and hearing difficulties.

If you only suffer from a mild cold, you can aid pressure modulation by holding your nose closed, gently pressing it and then swallowing. Chewing and yawning movements can additionally prompt the tiny muscles of the Eustachian tube to contract and thus open up the canal connecting your ear to your nose and throat. Nasal sprays facilitate this process, as they reduce swelling of the mucous membranes and thus improve air circulation.

These little tricks no longer work, however, if you suffer from a severe cold and clogged sinuses. If your head already feels like it is going to explode when you are on the ground, you should not fly. In the air, these symptoms will only be magnified. Ruptured ear drums as a result of pressure injuries can lead to complex conditions of the auditory system and even result in hearing loss.

Sometimes and against their better judgment, even flight personnel misjudge their own fitness to fly and board the plane despite suffering from a cold. Often these employees then lose their medical certification and subsequently their job due to an ear injury.

These examples show how difficult it is to correctly judge your own fitness to fly, even as an adult. Special caution is therefore required when it comes to babies and small children. Always consult a physician to avoid lasting damage.

Generally speaking, infants and small children suffering from a cold are not fit to fly! But even healthy children should be woken up prior to descent to support the necessary pressure modulation through chewing and yawning movements (aided by pacifiers or water, for example).

Germs & Co.

Contrary to colds which are often downplayed, possible germs on board are usually overestimated. Since passengers travel together in an enclosed space for hours on end, air in the cabin needs to be constantly renewed. During this process, it is filtered and fed back into the cabin, enriched with fresh air. In doing so, the systems effectively remove viruses and bacteria from the air and transport them out of the cabin via the outgoing air.

The *World Health Organization* WHO confirms that the risk of contracting an infectious disease on board an aircraft is low. Travelers who sit in the same area of the plane can infect each other, but – according to WHO – the risk is no higher than in any other situation or means of public transport where people are close together.

Nonetheless, there are a few areas on a plane that get touched with particular frequency and where pathogens therefore tend to accumulate. Typical contagion points include headrests, folding tables, seat pockets, lavatory door handles, toilet flush handles and sinks. What you can do to keep the germs away, to protect yourself and others?

Drinking sufficient amounts of water will prevent your mucous membranes from becoming dry, as this alone will reduce the number of pathogens that can proliferate. Medical experts suggest regularly washing your hands with soap, avoiding touching your face as far as possible, not placing food on the tabletop in front of you and, if needed cleaning areas that come into contact with your skin with a disinfecting wipe. It is also a good idea to have a face mask in your hand luggage and to have a sufficient supply of tissues on you.

In some countries, it is a legal requirement to remove any insects from an aircraft before landing *(disinsection)*. Not being native to the country of destination, these blind passengers could introduce new pathogens. Since the crew spread pesticides from spray bottles during this process, passengers often falsely conclude that this serves to kill germs. However, national health authorities, and not the cabin crew, govern the necessity of this measure.

Planning & Organization

The logistics behind air travel

Many individual components are required to ensure smooth and profitable airplane travel. Every flight involves considerable costs and airlines employ various strategies to keep them low. Cooperations and long-term contracts allow for procurement, maintenance, fuel and catering discounts.

In order to be economical, it is necessary to utilize individual aircraft as efficiently as possible by offering attractive fares and investing in a route network that is appealing to passengers. In the framework of so-called *yield management*, airlines constantly look for new solutions to optimally utilize their planes, taking into account purchase customers are willing to meet higher costs. Potential and new clientele are encouraged to buy tickets by offering various booking classes and fare models. Those who wish to book their vacation early on are much more price-conscious than someone who needs to get to a business appointment at short notice. The benefits of bonus schemes furthermore ensure air passenger loyalty.

When calculating prices, certain airlines even overbook their planes. They sell more tickets than there are seats on board on purpose and deliberately run the risk of some people not being able to embark on their journey. Statistics and data collection as part of yield management help airlines determine the average number of people who will not show up for their booked flight. Based on this, the respective number of additional tickets is made available for sale. These strategies do not always work and leave behind disgruntled customers who then need to be compensated.

The number of daily flights is likewise subject to strategic considerations. The less waiting time an aircraft spends on the ground, the more economical its operation will be for the airline. After all, while an airplane is on the ground it is not making any money. This often leads to arrival and departure times being scheduled so close together that individual delays can affect the entire day's flight schedule.

Extensive logistics and coordination are also required in the field of human resource management. Generally, the amount of training airlines are legally required to conduct is very high. Flight attendants and pilots, in particular, must be constantly trained and new recruits are integrated into ongoing operations. Duty and rest time regulations must be controlled and taken into account when drawing up duty rosters.

When it comes to operations, flight dispatchers take care of the submission and approval of the flight plan long before the scheduled departure. The flight plan is sent to a central collection point where all activities and aircraft movements across the entire airspace are coordinated before local air traffic controllers schedule the actual arrivals and departures.

Prior to flight, the cockpit crew receives up-to-date weather data for the entire route, calculates the fuel requirement and inspects the aircraft from the outside (*outside check*). Flight attendants coordinate service procedures and prepare the cabin for its next use. The cleaning staff cleans the inside of the aircraft and empties the seat pockets, while the catering team delivers the meals (if any are served) as well as magazines and items that increase passenger comfort. In the meantime, luggage and any travel bags are transported by a fully automated baggage sorting system through the security check to a waiting baggage cart or several containers. The ground service staff manually load and unload the aircraft. At the same time, there is the first call for passengers to start boarding.

What happens when aircraft are on the ground?

After landing at the destination airport, aircraft crews usually have about thirty to fifty minutes to prepare the plane for the return or onward flight. At low-cost airlines, this time window is often smaller.

After seeing off the passengers (on certain airlines the pilot himself stands at the exit), one of the two pilots leaves the aircraft and performs a visual inspection of the plane's exterior looking for visible damage to the engines, landing flaps and landing gear. At the same time, the pilot who remained in the cockpit programs the navigation computer for the return or onward flight and calculates how much fuel will be required. The latter depends on the weight of the aircraft, the number of passengers and the planned route, including a sufficient reserve.

While the plane is being refueled, cleaning personnel and the rest of the crew make sure that its interior is ready for the next passengers. They clean the seats, floor and lavatory, empty garbage bags and prepare the galley. They also provide magazines and other on-board equipment. Once these tasks have been completed, the next passengers are called for boarding.

Shortly before departure, the »ramp agent« hands the flight weather report and so-called »loadsheet« over to the pilots, the latter containing all important flight data such as weight calculations, cargo and number of passengers. »Ramp agents« are responsible for coordinating the aircraft's handling on the ground and monitoring the various tasks to make sure all required jobs are performed within the specified time window.

Standing in the corridor to the cockpit after passengers have boarded, they can often be identified by their high-visibility vest and a clipboard under their arm. Before the doors are closed, the »ramp agent« leaves the aircraft.

This marks the end of the last preparations for the cockpit crew so that the push-back of the aircraft from its parking position onto the taxiway can be carried out by an apron vehicle once the clearance to start the engines has been given. Finally, the »ramp agent« signals with a hand gesture that the aircraft wheels are not chocked anymore and the pins are removed. As soon as a clearance is obtained from the tower the aircraft is permitted to start taxiing towards the runway.

Aircraft de-icing

Just like your car in your driveway, aircraft need to be de-iced in wintry conditions. Even small amounts of snow and ice increase a plane's total weight. Moreover, frozen water alters its surfaces, which impedes its aerodynamic properties. To prevent this from happening, the wings, rudders and other moving control surfaces are sprayed down with a mix of glycol and water before take-off.

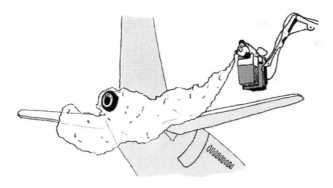

Depending on the aircraft's size, this treatment can last a few minutes which may lead to delays. Once the de-icing liquid has been applied, however, the plane needs to take off within a certain time window. If it is postponed too long, the liquid's effect can diminish and ice can build up once again on the wings. In such cases, the de-icing process must be repeated, which is very costly for the airline.

During the flight, the aircraft systems prevent the formation of ice. Warm air from the engines, for instance, is routed into the interior of the wings to heat them up from the inside and prevent ice from building up. These technologies allow aircraft to land even in wintry conditions without difficulty.

What are slots?

»Slots« are the time windows available for a plane's take-off or landing. This allocation helps to regulate and control traffic flow, as airports only have a limited number of gates and parking spaces, as well as runways, which also restricts the number of inbound and outbound flights they can handle.

High-traffic airports allocate fixed »slots« for scheduled flights that continuously take place on the same day of the week and the same time. However, these take-off and landing rights are not guaranteed. If the weather does not allow the scheduled traffic volumes or if the airport is struggling with delays, a new time window is assigned instead of the usual »slot«. Even an approaching thunderstorm can seriously disrupt regular operations. Capacity bottlenecks can also happen along the flight route. This sometimes results in restrictions to incoming and outgoing flights.

Time delays are a nuisance for all those involved, but new »slots« due to bad weather or airspace congestion are not assigned by the airlines. Changes to time slots prolong not only your journey but also the workday of the entire aircraft crew. It is therefore also in the interest of airlines to reduce delays to a minimum.

Aircraft maintenance intervals

Planes are checked for visible damage or faults before every flight. All pilots ensure the perfect condition of their aircraft. Furthermore, qualified maintenance personnel perform *line maintenance* tasks during which tires, brakes and engines are checked and the oil level, hydraulic fluid and technical systems are inspected.

Ongoing checks, combined with extensive component maintenance, increase the longevity of the materials and are thus of immense importance to airlines. Apart from these daily checks, there are four different maintenance procedures of different levels.

Regular »A-checks« are often performed overnight. This check is similar to having a thorough service performed on your car. Only a few aircraft are subject to »B-checks« which build on the aforementioned regular inspections.

Next in the hierarchy are »C-checks«, for which the aircraft is taken out of service for one to two weeks. During this check, technicians dismantle individual parts and subject them to structural and functional checks. This allows maintenance teams to also access areas that are hard to reach. In addition, it is a good opportunity to perform technical upgrades.

The by far most comprehensive checks are »D-checks« which take place roughly every eight years and take about two months to complete. Over the course of countless man hours, the aircraft is then stripped down to the last bolt. Every part is examined for wear and replaced, if needed. Technical systems are repaired and sometimes modernized. Airlines often use this opportunity to thoroughly overhaul the interior; to give the on-board kitchen, lavatories and floors a new sheen.

Once work is completed, the plane is reassembled, meticulously tested and receives a new coat of paint before it is put back into service. Considering the scope of these maintenance efforts, it is no exaggeration to speak of a completely new aircraft once completed.

If any deficiencies are reported between the individual maintenance intervals, they are entered by the cockpit crew in the aircraft's logbook. Published by the manufacturer, *minimum equipment lists* specify whether the aircraft is still fit to fly and if so, how many days are left until the next maintenance deadline. Once the component has been checked and replaced and the aircraft's normal state has been restored, the completion of this task is confirmed in the logbook. This method gives every aircraft a transparent technical resume.

The Aircraft

How do planes fly?

You have probably watched an airplane take off before. Its engines produce thrust seemingly effortlessly and gently lift the multiple-ton behemoth off the ground and continuously higher up into the air. Only a few minutes later, the plane has reached its cruising altitude and crosses entire continents.

How is that possible? How do aircraft stay in the air? Every object is drawn towards the center of the earth by gravity. An aircraft's aerodynamically shaped wings counter these physical forces when a suction effect is applied to these wings at an appropriate speed. The plane is literally pulled up. Both the shape and length of the wings are vital when it comes to maintaining sufficient uplift. Their design is based on nature and reminiscent of birds' wings. In order to achieve flying speed, sufficient volumes of surrounding air have to pass over and under the wings. The engines, meanwhile, provide the necessary thrust and forward momentum. Natural air resistance is used as braking support to slow the aircraft down. If you have ever ridden a bicycle against a headwind, you know how strong this drag can be.

Long before an aircraft embarks on its first flight, the manufacturers make immensely complex calculations to find the performance characteristics that will make it fly most efficiently. Models allow them to test the results in wind tunnels. One of the prime considerations is to keep fuel consumption as low as possible. This is not only important to protect the climate but also in the interest of the airlines' price calculations. Without a doubt, the wing design and the use of modern materials produce large savings potential in this regard.

What are winglets?

»Winglets« (various manufacturers also call them *wingtip fences, sharklets, blended* or *raked wingtips*) are attachments at the tip of the wings that are usually curved upwards. They are designed to go on the ends of wings, where they reduce so-called induced drag. The latter is responsible for air turbulences that are created by pressure differences between the top and underside of the wings and disrupt the plane's aerodynamics.

Attaching these »winglets« reduces fuel consumption by about three to five percent, which makes air traffic cheaper and at the same time better for the environment. Older aircraft can be retrofitted with »winglets« and many airlines have already commissioned this upgrade.

Rudders are not just for boats

When steering a plane, pilots adjust three axes during flight. Contrary to a car, an aircraft allows for three-dimensional movements and changes of direction.

The vertical axis runs through the plane from top to bottom, the horizontal axis from its nose to its tail and the lateral one between the tips of the wings. The point where they all meet forms the plane's center of gravity. The aircraft is steered around an axis with moving flaps also called rudders. Similar to paddles in the water, they allow the pilot to change course precisely.

The ailerons are located at the outer edge of the wings. They allow the aircraft to »roll« around its horizontal axis. To initiate a left turn, the control wheel or control stick is moved to the left. This lifts the ailerons on the left wing, thus increasing the air drag. At the same time, the ailerons on the right wing are lowered, increasing uplift. The rudders on the wings thus move in opposition.

So-called elevators take care of the airplane's »pitch« around the lateral axis. Pushing the control wheel forward makes the plane start to descend. The elevators at the back of the aircraft are thereby lowered. In order to initiate an ascent, on the other hand, the pilot pulls on the control element, making the elevators move upwards.

Two foot pedals are used to make the plane move around its vertical axis. When the pilot presses the pedal on the right with his right foot, the corresponding rudder on the back also turns right. In turn, the left pedal – pressed by the left foot – turns the rudder to the left. Up in the air, this movement supports the aircraft when making turns. These rudders are even more important when it comes to landing: they allow the plane to be brought down precisely on the centerline of the runway. The stronger the crosswinds are, the more these rudder pedals will be used.

Propeller engines

Contrary to airliners powered by jet engines, passenger airplanes equipped with turboprop engines are often seen as loud, old and unsafe by the public. However, this type of engine is much better than its reputation suggests and is by no means outdated. This fact is proven by the regular introduction of new versions of such planes that are just as safe as jet-powered ones.

In direct comparison, turboprop planes might be slower but also use less fuel over short distances. This and other properties sometimes make them the only feasible choice. Without propeller planes, certain airports and islands could not be serviced at all, especially those with short runways. Due to their lower numbers of seats, they are furthermore used on low-demand routes. This allows airlines to also service routes on which the use of larger aircraft would simply be uneconomical.

Full engine speed ahead

A passenger plane's engines perform many different functions. First and foremost, they deliver the thrust that the aircraft needs to lift off and reach the required cruising speed. The systems work reliably and fault-free, even in bad weather. Most commercial planes are equipped with turbine or jet engines designed for high altitude use. These engines have a complex structure and allow the plane to maintain high speeds over long distances.

The visible outer part of an aircraft engine consists of *fans* with a spintop-shaped cover, called a *spinner*, in the middle. Usually white on a black background, a spiral is painted onto this cover. Even when working in high-noise areas, this allows ground crew to spot at a glance whether the engine is running or not.

How does this engine work?

Behind the fans, the air flow is divided into two streams. One airstream is guided into a compressor where it squeezes the air and increases its pressure. Extracting the entire air from the interior of a car and pressing it into a washing machine would create a similar compressive force. This process slows down and heats up the airstream which is then fed into the combustion chamber. Fuel is injected there and combusted. The combustion chamber is a hellish place with temperatures of more than 3,650 degrees Fahrenheit (2,000 degrees Celsius). From this area, exhaust gases are emitted with speeds of over 620 miles an hour (1,000 kilometers an hour), which hit the turbine and make it spin. The energy thus created drives the fans and compressor, while the hot air cools and escapes through the thrust nozzle at the rear of the engine.

However, most of the thrust comes from the second airstream. It guides enormous volumes of air along the engine walls and serves to cool the compressor, combustion chamber and turbine. The larger the engine's diameter, the more air volume it can process. This is why the size of the engines is directly related to the size of the aircraft. When exiting at the back, these huge amounts of air create the thrust required to propel the aircraft forward. The higher the speed of this process, the faster the aircraft will fly.

However, the engines also have other tasks and are connected to more technical components in the aircraft. For example, the airstream also drives additional generators that produce the power used by the on-board electrical systems. This is also how the hydraulic pumps are set in motion that make the landing flaps extend and retract. The pressurized air needed to control the air conditioning system, the pressurized cabin as well as the wing and engine de-icing systems is also generated by the engines.

Since the engines are of crucial importance, they have a particularly sturdy construction and are equipped with designated safety features. For instance, they have their own independent fire extinguishing systems and are thoroughly tested before being approved for flight operation. Above all, the manufacturing teams focus on how the engine will behave in the event of damage in order to implement appropriate safety measures. During these tests, one of the fans is blown off at full rotational speed, for example. The engine has passed the test if all parts remain in the cowling.

Material sucked into the engine on the ground as well as collisions with birds in the air pose a constant danger to the integrity of the engines. To simulate this situation, frozen chickens and similar artificial objects are shot into running engines using a »chicken cannon«. The conditions are equal to a collision with a live animal. In optimally functioning engines, the fans first push the bird to the edge of the inner casing, from where the second airstream pushes it out to the rear of the engine. However, the impact is so severe that the bird will not survive. In many cases, this design prevents serious damage. If the engine still causes problems, it is switched off while the aircraft is still in the air.

This may sound frightening, but the second engine is fully capable of assuming all flight operation functions on its own without restrictions. In most cases, however, the pilots still decide to perform an unscheduled safety landing as the full extent of the damage can be better assessed during an inspection on the ground.

The hidden auxiliary power unit

In addition to the main engines, the most common aircraft models are equipped with an *auxiliary power unit* (APU) in the tail section. It is used to ensure a power supply on the ground when the main engines are switched off. Exiting gases causing a heat haze at the rear of the aircraft show when the auxiliary power unit is running.

If the auxiliary power unit experiences a technical defect or if its use is prohibited at an airport due to noise restrictions, a *ground power unit* (GPU) can be used to feed electric energy into the on-board systems. In this case, the aircraft is connected to the airport via a special plug.

The second important task of the auxiliary power unit is to enable the powering of the actual main engines. It delivers the pressurized air required to increase the rotational speed of the turbine to around 10 to 20 percent of its power before the main engine is able to ignite and run on its own. After that, the auxiliary power unit is shut off as it has no function during the actual flight and is neither required to produce on-board power nor to drive the air conditioning system.

What does the black box do?

Better known as »black boxes«, flight recorders are technical devices that record all relevant flight data. Its English name, however, is misleading. To make them easier to find after a plane crash, »black boxes« are not black at all, but red or bright orange instead. Due to their sturdy stainless steel or titanium casing, »black boxes« are capable of withstanding impacts equal to 3,400 times their own weight and surviving temperatures of up to

2,000 degrees Fahrenheit (1,100 degrees Celsius). Moreover, the »black box« is waterproof and can be located at depths of up to 20,000 feet (6,000 meters). So that flight recorders can be found in even the most remote regions, these devices transmit a signal every second for at least thirty days.

The »black box» usually consists of two units: the *cockpit voice recorder* and a *flight data recorder*. The latter records some 3,000 different aircraft system parameters. Above all, it records engine data in great detail. On top of that, it provides information on speed, flight altitude, heading, pitch, weather events and warning signals for the last twenty-five flight hours. Aircraft configurations such as the position of the landing flaps or landing gear are also recorded, as are all rudder movements.

The voice recorder, on the other hand, records all conversations in the cockpit over the course of the last two hours. High-quality microphones not only allow the complete recording of all words uttered in the cockpit but also capture radio communication. There is another interesting fact: all operating and control elements in the cockpit emit their own distinct sounds that are also recorded. This enables specialists to reconstruct in detail what button was pushed when examining a damage event. In order to prevent all interference with the recordings, data manipulation or even the destruction of »black boxes«, they are installed in an inaccessible place in the rear of the aircraft.

Fuel dumping

Small clouds often appear at the rear edges of the wings during landing. These are simply water molecules that become visible at high humidity but are often mistaken for dumped fuel. In fact, fuel dumping is only permitted in specific emergency and danger situations. An unavoidable circumstance must warrant this action which is governed by strict rules. Furthermore, airlines are not interested in routinely dumping fuel. After all, they go to great lengths to save fuel and dumping it would incur considerable financial losses. So why is this option even available?

Only a few types of aircraft are technically actually able to dump fuel in the air. The most common short and medium-range aircraft are not equipped with this facility. In the event of an emergency they are capable of landing quickly due to their small fuel tanks and low total weight. However, on long-haul aircraft, the weight difference between full tanks at departure and almost empty tanks at arrival is so great that they are incapable of touching down again immediately after take-off due to their high weight. Moreover, this would put the landing gear and aircraft structure under enormous strain and compromise a safe landing.

However, medical emergencies may require the aircraft to quickly return to its departure airport. Ensuring the potentially life-saving treatment of a passenger on the ground does not allow the pilots to fly around for hours just to empty the tanks. This is why some long-haul aircraft are technically equipped with the option of dumping their fuel in the air.

A device then atomizes the content of the tank, ensuring its immediate evaporation in the atmosphere. Only a small percentage actually reaches the ground. Since such cases of fuel dumping are extremely rare, should it be necessary the environmental impact can be assumed to be pretty low.

Brake, brake, brake!

The speed of an aircraft is controlled by the output of its engines. Reducing their thrust reduces the flight speed. Additionally, the pilots can extend so-called speed brakes or spoilers on the upper side of the wings. These increase drag, slowing the plane down. Passengers sitting with a view over the wings can watch this process closely, especially during landing.

On the approach to landing, the so-called landing flaps allow slow flight. First, the aircraft touches down on the runway with its main landing gear. Immediately followed by the nose landing gear. Its tires create rolling resistance that also has a braking effect. At this point, the pilots activate the wheel brakes using foot pedals in the cockpit. The speed brakes are fully extended and reverse thrust is activated. During this process, the engine airstream is reversed to make the air flow out of the front and help slow down the aircraft. This braking option relieves the wheel brakes and significantly shortens the braking distance. It therefore takes less than 100 seconds for an aircraft to come to a complete stop.

Landing gear and tires

Aircraft's sturdy landing gear and tires are secret weightlifting champions. After all, they carry the plane's entire weight. Apart from take-off and landing, during which landing gear and tires are indispensable, they make sure the plane is easy to maneuver at airports and – with their shock absorbers – serve as a kind of spacer to prevent parts of the plane from getting damaged by touching the ground.

Contrary to car tires, aircraft tires are not filled with air but nitrogen, protecting the tubeless tires from overheating. Every tire is several layers thick and weighs 220 to 330 pounds (100 to

150 kilograms), depending on its size. The material is extra tough and can easily withstand high temperature fluctuations. Due to the not inconsiderable rubber abrasion during take-off and landing, however, the tires wear. After all, depending on type, aircraft touch down with average speeds of 110 to 140 knots (200 to 260 kilometers per hour). The forces acting on the landing gear in the process are lowered and cushioned by the tires and shock absorbers.

The tread and tire pressure are checked before every flight to identify defects early on. If there are doubts over the reliable function of a tire or if damage has occurred, the affected wheel is replaced immediately. However, aircraft tires are not thrown away after use. Instead, they can be reused several times following a thorough reconditioning.

Landing gear is entirely disassembled and completely overhauled on average every eight years during the so-called »D-Check«. Using state-of-the-art technology, minute cracks and signs of corrosion can be detected and repaired if needed before the structure is reinstalled on the aircraft after another test.

The landing gear is controlled from the cockpit. Electronic sensors monitor the hydraulically controlled system and indicate whether the landing gear is extended or retracted on a designated indicator panel. Using color-coded displays, the pilot can then determine the respective position and adjust it by pulling a lever.

In case the main system experiences a technical defect, commercial aircraft are equipped with a simple yet ingenious safety measure: the cockpit also features a manually controlled override that the pilots can use to unlock the landing gear in the event of an emergency. Gravity then takes care of the rest – the landing gear is simply pulled downwards by its own weight and locks in place. This method ensures safe landing, even in the highly unlikely event of a defective hydraulic system during the flight.

Flying & Entertainment

Aviation: then and now

A 4,000-year-old Sumerian seal found during excavations, depicting the shepherd *Etana* riding an eagle, proves that humans have been fascinated by the concept of flying since time immemorial. It is the oldest known depiction of a human taking to the skies. Myths, legends, fairy tales and stories about heavenly bodies and flying creatures abound in almost all cultures. However, it took humans thousands of years before they were able to actually consider flying from a technical perspective.

Back in the 15th century, Italian artist and jack-of-all-trades Leonardo da Vinci famously created sketches of a propeller-driven device evoking modern Helicopters. It was not actually capable of flying but da Vinci's ideas provided great inspiration for other inventors. Many haphazard attempts to get objects, animals and humans airborne were made over the course of the following centuries, with most of them ending in tragedy. A thorough understanding of aerodynamics was lacking.

It would take until the late 19th century before significant progress in the development towards modern aviation was made by German aviation pioneer Otto Lilienthal. Lilienthal studied birds in flight and attempted to optimally apply the knowledge of aerodynamics that he gathered to his own flying apparatus. Courageous enough to test his own designs, he succeeded in carrying out several gliding flights. In the early 20th century, brothers Wilbur and Orville Wright from the USA were able to build on his insights, with inventions involving controlled motorized flight. Together with other inventors, they designed machines capable of flying, improved aerodynamics and controls and thus heralded the new age of aviation.

The first half of the 20th century was rife with further pioneering ideas and inventions, leading to the growth of a significant new industrial sector. A competition for planes that could fly ever faster and higher also ensued. Alongside civil uses, military interests soon became significant drivers of technical progress. Aircraft shapes became more varied and many different materials were tested for their suitability for aircraft construction.

The maiden flight of the British »de Havilland DH 106 Comet« in 1949 marked the beginning of the age of the serial production of commercial jet airliners. It was the birth of industrial aircraft manufacturing as we know it today.

Nineteen years later, another sensational technical breakthrough was made when the Soviet »Tupolev Tu-144« became the first passenger plane to break the sound barrier – two months before the much better known »Concorde« achieved the same feat when it took to the skies for the first time on 2nd March 1969. Due to high ticket prices, flights on supersonic planes were restricted to a small group of privileged people, before these flights were abandoned altogether in 2003.

Quite a different airplane also made news in 1969. US manufacturer Boeing released its immensely successful »Boeing 747« which would remain the largest passenger aircraft in the world for a long time. Equipped with four engines and two passenger decks, it was nicknamed »jumbo jet« in reference to the famed king of elephants. The »Boeing 747« remained the quintessential wide-bodied aircraft until 2005, when it had to step down in favor of a European rival. Up to this day, the »Airbus A380« bears the title of the largest passenger aircraft ever built.

Today, technical innovations in the aviation industry rarely focus on enlarging the aircraft. Instead, they concentrate on environmental protection and the goal of making flying more cost-effective, efficient and environmentally friendly. However, until alternative propulsion systems become available, there is a need for measures to upgrade existing fleets. For example, there are attempts to reduce the harmful emissions of the latest generations of engines, while many airports also have restrictions, even flight bans for older types of aircraft. After all, every effort helps to reduce excessive CO_2 emissions that contribute to rapid global warming.

More and more airlines inform their passengers during booking about their ecological footprint, for example by means of an emissions calculator that calculates the current fuel consumption of the flight. Apart from these efforts to raise awareness, however, new ideas and concepts are still required to enable forthcoming generations to fly to all parts of the planet.

Freedom above the clouds

Air traffic is very well interlinked and there is hardly a place on earth that cannot be reached by means of direct or transfer routes. Even remote regions can be accessed by airplane or helicopter.

International communities of nations work together closely to ensure the system works everywhere. The so-called *Freedoms of the Air* established the legal framework for flying across national borders without problems. What rules govern flights through foreign airspace?

Generally, airspace can be used without restrictions unless local laws contain regulations to the contrary. In accordance with this, every nation makes independent decisions regarding its sovereign territory. International overflight rights can be restricted or revoked at any time for safety reasons.

Airspace potentially hazardous for aircraft is called a *danger area*. More often than not, military activities such as air combat drills are the reason for such restrictions. Since these are restricted locally and in terms of altitude, however, they can be overflown or bypassed easily.

When it comes to protecting air traffic and facilities on the ground, *restricted areas* are established. Flying across such special areas is subject to conditions. These can include maintaining a certain minimum altitude or adhering to time windows. This makes it easier to protect special structures such as nuclear power plants and facilities of importance to religious groups or tourists.

Prohibited areas can be established to completely keep out civilian air traffic. In the event of war, airspace can be closed off permanently in certain areas. During a state visit or a similarly sensitive event, these bans are only imposed for certain periods of time. In some countries the difference between restricted and prohibited areas is blurred. In both cases, entering or flying over such an area can be strictly forbidden.

By the way: private individuals are obligated by law to not restrict flights over their gardens, homes or agricultural spaces at any time. In return, measures to prevent noise pollution are implemented, for instance by means of specially scheduled flight routes and legally required minimum altitudes. To ease the noise burden on residents living near airports, steeper approach angles and other noise-reducing flight maneuvers are increasingly used.

What is jetlag?

On a long-haul flight, you cross many times zones and a few hours after departing, you find yourself not only in a different country but also an entirely new daily cycle. The fact that your day is cut short or extended completely throws your internal clock off and day and nighttime hours seem to be out of kilter with your daily routine.

Passengers are usually struck particularly hard by these effects on eastbound flights. This is due to the earth's eastward rotation which leads to your day being shortened. On flights that take off late in the evening or during the night, you get significantly fewer hours of darkness. If it has not happened already, this is when the altered daily structure really kicks in, in this case due to lack of sleep. On the plus side, you »gain« a few hours when flying from Europe to the USA, for instance. When flying westwards, there are more sunlight hours which most people tolerate better.

The human body finds it difficult to tolerate quick time zone changes since they can significantly shift one's familiar sleep-wake cycle. The results can include fatigue, sleeping disorders, lack of appetite, as well as mood swings and physical complaints. Our digestive system is particularly susceptible. It is adapted to our country of origin's time zone and works accordingly. Your stomach and bowels need some time to get used to the new circadian rhythm. A rule of thumb is that your body will require one day of acclimatization for every time zone crossed.
When flying from Dubai in the United Arab Emirates to Kuala Lumpur in Malaysia, for instance, you will cross four time zones, meaning that you can expect to need four days of acclimatization.

However, the effects of jetlag are highly individual and are not determined by your state of health or age. Babies are an exception: as their internal clock is not fully developed yet, no day/night cycle is established in the first weeks of their lives.

Alleviating jetlag

For biological reasons, you cannot fully escape jetlag. Nevertheless, there are a few strategies you can use to increase your wellbeing and alleviate its effects. Every traveler is exhausted after a long-haul flight, because both the long periods of sitting and acclimatizing to a new time zone are a strain on our bodies. This is why you should allow for sufficient rest periods on the day of your arrival. At the same time, it is advisable to adapt to the local time as quickly as possible.

Relaxation exercises can help your body let go of everyday stress and enter relaxation mode. Soothing music, an easy-to-read book or a hot bath before going to bed can support this effect. You should also ensure an optimal room climate and darken your room to allow your body to get a good night's sleep. Store items that remind you of your work, as well as electronic devices, in a different room and out of sight. If you still find it difficult to fall asleep, a walk can help.
Ideally, get up at the same time every day in your new time zone. This establishes a daily rhythm and helps your body adapt. It is also advisable to refrain from all additional negative habits like eating fatty and sugary food, as well as smoking or drinking alcohol during the acclimatization period.

Business travelers usually do not have a lot of time to recuperate at their destination. Appointments are often scheduled for a time immediately after arrival. There are little tricks that help you fight fatigue, albeit they only work for a limited period of time. Among others, your circadian rhythm is controlled by the hormone melatonin which is produced by the body at dusk and leads to fatigue. Light, on the other hand, inhibits the production of this sleep hormone. For this reason, if you have to keep an important appointment immediately after arrival and do not have time to recuperate, you should spend as much time in the sun as possible to draw new energy.

With advancing age, our bodies produce less melatonin and we need less and less sleep. This is why older travelers can ease time zone stress by means of conscious relaxation, even without prolonged deep sleep phases. Only if your journey takes less than three days can it make sense to stick to your familiar rhythm. If this is not possible, prolonged periods of rest and relaxation are once again the key to alleviating the effects of jetlag.

The (missing) on-board menu

Catering on board is an important aspect of a flight for many passengers. Being served food and beverages is a long-standing tradition in the aviation industry. In the early days of commercial aviation, when airplanes were not yet a means of mass transport, food was used to demonstrate the exclusivity of a flight.

At the same time, it served as a signal to all those flying for the first time that fear of flying was unfounded. After all, how can flying be dangerous if something as mundane and familiar as eating is possible on board? This basic notion still applies today. Eating not only distracts from one's anxieties and worries, it also increases our wellbeing and personal contentment.

From the perspective of aviation medicine, the importance of on-board meals is about more than just satisfying our natural feeling of hunger and thirst. The longer a flight lasts, the higher the risk of suffering from dehydration, as the dry air on board dehydrates the body more quickly than on the ground. Lack of sustenance also comes with its own problems. In connection with turbulence, physical wellbeing can rapidly deteriorate. Decreasing blood sugar levels can cause us to sweat, develop sudden cravings or poor concentration. All of that could make passengers increasingly frustrated or even aggressive. Neither of these are desirable characteristics nor good news on an aircraft.

Many passengers would like a meal even on short flights. However, cabin crew only serve little snacks, if that, on short-haul flights. Depending on the airline and price category of your ticket, they might be included or subject to a surcharge. Including entire menus in the ticket price is only common on long-haul flights. Some airlines strive to provide particularly high levels of service on board. After all, in-flight catering is one of the few aspects that allow passengers to compare competing companies. A passenger is not in a position to evaluate proper aircraft maintenance but can by all means judge the catering, served by friendly flight attendants.

Considerable logistic efforts go into aircraft catering. Food is prepared in commercial kitchens, frozen or packed for immediate transport. Apart from main meals such as breakfast, lunch and dinner, the range of food on offer also includes various entremets. On top of that, meal selection differs greatly between the individual categories of Economy, Business and First Class. Some companies offer special children's menus as an option.

Airlines alone decide what they serve on board and usually they choose menus favored by the majority of travelers from a myriad of offers. Commercial kitchens and catering companies are also capable of satisfying special wishes and creating tasty vegetarian and vegan dishes. Even dietary rules governed by religious beliefs can be adhered to upon request. No matter what dishes airlines opt for, highly fragrant ones are usually not on the menu.

As the departure approaches, food trolleys are filled and sorted on the ground and their entire content is counted and checked, as flight attendants have neither the space nor the time for this on board. Computer-aided programs monitor this process and ensure trouble-free procedures along the entire delivery chain. Special vehicles lift the prepared catering into commercial airplanes, after which it is stored in the aircraft's galley. Once mealtime has arrived, the cabin crew warms the meals up in the oven and puts them on the trolleys. These last preparations are made swiftly since passengers like to be served their meals as simultaneously as possible. Following a specified process and on the basis of pre-coordinated task sharing, the cabin crew then distributes food and beverages.

Mealtime rules for the crew

Aircraft crews work shifts which means that there is no daily routine and no specified mealtime. In order to stay healthy despite this, a responsible approach to fatty, sweet and high-calorie food is essential. Flight personnel's own health is paramount to be able to deal with the physical demands of flying. After all, their fitness to fly depends on their nutrition and eating behavior and every crew member knows that.

To keep the risk of food poisoning to a minimum, pilots and flight attendants are obliged to refrain from eating raw meat or fish. Some airlines even require their cockpit crews to take in a variety of meals during a flight. In this case, pilots have a choice of meals. Although it is very rare for catering companies to have contaminated ingredients in their meals, mistakes cannot be ruled out. Should a pilot become sick due to food that is off, the other one can safely fly the plane and even land it on their own at the destination airport.

High-flying entertainment

Entertaining guests on board with multi-media content is more than just a service provided by the airlines. Even if most passengers nowadays come to expect this kind of equipment on board, it was introduced for psychological and sociological reasons.

Even a single passenger's misconduct can have unpleasant consequences for them and other passengers. It is deemed that this potential risk increases the longer the flight takes. The airlines therefore strive to curb any possibility of boredom.

As far back as 1921, the US airline »Aeromarine Airways« was the first one to show a movie on board its seaplane. Eleven years later, a TV broadcast was shown for the first time on board an aircraft owned by Californian »Western Airlines«. Many years would pass until headphones made their way into aircraft cabins in 1963.

Other milestones were the first video games in 1975, followed by individually controlled audio systems in 1985. The first video entertainment systems built into the seat were introduced in 1988. Creating a new trend, German »Lufthansa« became the world's first airline to offer broadband Internet on a long-haul flight in 2003.

In addition to traditional entertainment offerings, some airlines offer *Moving Map Systems* that show detailed information about the flight's progression and allow passengers to trace the aircraft's route. The data required for this is supplied by the plane's navigation computer, allowing for real-time images. Apart from its current position, passengers are able to view information on their screens about the flight route, duration, and outside temperature, as well as cruising altitude and speed.

For the aviation industry, these varied entertainment options always mean a compromise between a marketable service and high installation and procurement costs. Continuous use of these electronic systems also involves regular maintenance and updates, which require additional human resources from the airline.

Units of measurement 101

Many fields of science, economics and technology use international units of measurement. Standardized units were established to allow all those involved to refer to the same numbers and to avoid cumbersome conversions. Based on the metric system, the *International System of Units* (SI) is the most common. Although the International Civil Aviation Organization ICAO recommended this very system of units for international use, it could not be established in aviation. Instead, the industry works with other units of measurement that sometimes differ from country to country. Strap yourself in! It could get a little confusing now!

Altimeters can be set to two different units of air pressure, *hectopascal* (hPa), a unit used by most of the world's nations, or *inch of mercury* (inHg), most common especially in the USA and Canada. Neither of them is used when it comes to measuring the air pressure in aircraft tires, however. For that, *pounds per square inch* (psi) is used instead.

In China and Russia, wind speeds are indicated to pilots in *meters per second* (m/s), while in the rest of the world *knots* (kn or kt) are more common, which is also the unit used as a parameter for flight speed on commercial airplanes. Smaller (propeller) aircraft, such as sports airplanes, often have an additional display showing *miles per hour* (mph). Contrary to this, some gliders display speed in *kilometers per hour* (km/h).

Internationally, distances are usually given in *feet* (ft), but China prefers to use the metric system and states flight distances in *meters* (m). And even in countries that usually use feet, ground visibility is most of the time measured in meters.

This potpourri of units is exacerbated further by the units of weight applied in the context of fueling. Depending on the type of plane, the country in which it is being fueled and what fuel calculation methods an airline uses, several reference values such as *US gallons* (gal), *pounds* (lb), *liters* (l) and *kilograms* (kg) are among the possibilities. This can result in aircraft instruments showing the fuel quantity on board in one unit, kerosene being filled in another and billed on the basis of a third.

Conversely, all parties seem to agree on using *Coordinated Universal Time* (UTC) whose center is based in London's Greenwich borough and from which all time zones are derived; and time differences calculated.

Navigation & the Cockpit

Waypoints and airways

In the early days of aviation, pilots would exclusively rely on their eyes to guide them. Mountains, distinctive shapes in the landscape, lakes, rivers, stars and other traditional navigational aids were used to determine location. Today, so-called inertial navigation systems record a range of aircraft data such as pitch angle, position and acceleration. Combined with the *Global Navigation Satellite System* (GNSS) the on-board systems are aware of the current position of the aircraft.

These systems can be used to calculate when and at which altitude a plane will fly over a certain point along the route. This accuracy ensures a safe and precise flight, even if outside visibility is compromised by bad weather or darkness. Passengers are often able to view the navigation computer's data on the aircraft's video screens in a simplified form.

Airspace is littered with waypoints, airways, crossings and one-ways. Aircraft do not fly around at random but follow specified routes. You can think about airspace as a three-dimensional highway network made up of several levels in the air. On its journey, an aircraft passes through several airspaces and must adhere to different rules in each one. One of these rules might be that one area may only be used by commercial planes but not by sports aircraft. These individual sectors are coordinated and monitored by air traffic controllers who are responsible for all aircraft currently en route in their defined airspace.

Just like traffic networks on the ground, airways have various entrance and exit points with individual references. Usually they consist of five letters made up of vowels and consonants, most often drawing on geographical reference points such as cities, mountains or lakes. However, they can also receive random names that are easy to understand on the radio.

In the USA, Florida's Orlando International Airport is known for assigning names connected to amusement parks in its vicinity, leading to waypoints such as MINEE, ALADN and BUGGZ in its approach area. These stand for the fictional characters *Minnie Mouse*, *Aladdin* and *Bugs Bunny*. CWRLD, of course, derives its name from the equally famous ocean theme park. Such memorable names, however, are rare among navigation points. Nonetheless, they serve their purpose and their uniqueness avoids confusion with waypoints that sound similar.

Bank angle and turns

The *artificial horizon* is the primary flight instrument to determine an aircraft's position in a three-dimensional space and perform precise horizontal and vertical maneuvers.

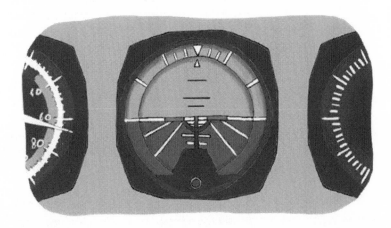

In relation to the aircraft's longitudinal axis, it shows the roll angle in degrees when flying a curve. Standard turns are performed with a bank angle of between 25 and 33 degrees. Pilots adhere to these values during every stage of the flight such as climb, cruising and descent.

Modern commercial aircraft monitor their own flight maneuvers. If a limit value is exceeded, an alarm signal is emitted in the cockpit. If a higher value is required, however, pilots can make their aircraft exceed these values. Aerodynamically, so-called steep turns with bank angles of more than 45 degrees are possible. Such excessive bank angles are not used on routine flights, however, as this would take passengers far beyond their comfort zone and rob them of all wellbeing.

The cockpit layout

You might have been able to catch a quick glimpse of the cockpit when getting on or off a plane and perhaps you have looked in awe at the colorful array and number of keys, buttons and levers seemingly arranged at random. And yet, cockpits are well thought out workspaces and the most common aircraft have similar layouts. Many pilots affectionately refer to their command center as their »office with a sunlit desk«.

The central pedestal between the pilots is home to the thrust lever, the selector for retracting and extending the landing flaps, as well as parts of the radio communication and navigation equipment. This is also where the part of the autopilot responsible for long-term flight planning (for instance programming flight routes) is located.

Situated directly in front of the pilots are several screens that show the flight attitude and the aircraft's operating limits, among others. For safety reasons, both pilots receive identical information on their screens to monitor the flight direction, altitude and speed. This also includes a pilot's most essential instrument, the artificial horizon. Flying in poor visibility or in darkness would be simply impossible without it.

A weather radar allows the pilots to detect thunderstorms along the route. Another part of route monitoring equipment is the collision warning device that reliably detects approaching aircraft and warns the crew early.

Located either directly in front of the pilot's upper body or to their side in the form of »sidestick«, the control wheels look slightly different depending on the aircraft type.

The overhead panel is home to technical systems used to control and monitor the on-board electronics, fuel tanks, interior and exterior lighting, the de-icing device, as well as smoke detectors and fire extinguishing equipment. All buttons and switches are labeled in addition to make it easier to tell them apart, avoiding confusion especially during stressful stages of the flight. The intensity of their backlighting can furthermore be adjusted on dusk and night flights.

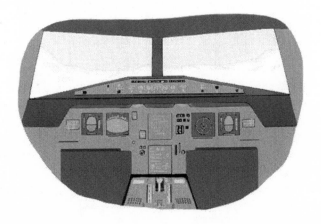

If a technical component or instrument should fail during the flight, the cockpit crew can switch to another one, since two or even three of all systems relevant to safety are available. If one of them becomes defective, a system of equal functionality can take over. Such eventualities are regularly trained in flight simulators to allow for every flight to be completed safely.

What does the autopilot do?

Many passengers think that modern cockpit crews simply switch on the autopilot and then lean back and spend the rest of the flight doing nothing. Needless to say, it is not as easy as that, but it is a fact that this technical device makes flying much more relaxed.

First and foremost, the autopilot serves as an automated control system that takes care of routine processes, thus taking some strain off the pilots. Among others, it is used to reach and maintain a precise cruising altitude. In addition, it is responsible for tasks related to navigation, following flight routes previously programmed that are monitored constantly and may have to be reprogrammed if and when needed. Programmed waypoints can change, for instance when air traffic controllers allow pilots to take shortcuts or require them to change direction.

At any point during the flight, the cockpit crew is ready to take control and deactivate the autopilot if required. After all, this technical device can neither follow the commands of air traffic controllers nor assess weather conditions, or make necessary decisions.

On the other hand, the autopilot is a particularly helpful device in stages of the flight that demand the full concentration of both pilots, for instance during landing approach or in bad weather conditions.

What is a jumpseat?

Passenger planes are equipped with several folding seats for cabin crew, usually located at the entry and exit points. Called »jumpseats« in aviation jargon, they are easy to identify and distinguish from passenger seats on the basis of their design.

They do not offer a lot of comfort since they are not intended to be sat in for long periods of time. Usually these seats are used during take-off and landing, as well as in the event of strong turbulence, ensuring the safety of the cabin crew.

Depending on the type of aircraft, the cockpit also features one or more »jumpseats«. They offer an optimal view of all instruments and allow the person sitting in them to observe the pilots during their work. If needed, this observation seat is used by an additional airline team member. Persons not belonging to the crew are only permitted to sit in this seat if both pilots give their consent and access is not prohibited by other factors.

This seat has always been one of the most sought-after on airplanes and makes many aviation enthusiasts go weak at the knees. Unfortunately, the cockpit »jumpseat« can neither be reserved nor booked and thus remains forever off limits to most people.

Weather & Turbulence

Wind direction during take-off and landing

As far as structurally permitted by an airport's geographical surroundings, runways are aligned with the main wind direction. During ongoing operations, runways can be used in both directions and they are numbered based on their orientation. Runway code »09« denotes an easterly runway, since east is at a 090 degree angle to north on the 360-degree compass rose. The final zero is simply omitted in the code. Clearly legible, both numbers are painted onto the asphalt surface at the beginning of the runway.

Ultimately, however, the current wind direction determines what direction is used for take-off and landing and that can change several times over the course of a day. For safety reasons, the use of runways currently occupied by another aircraft is prohibited. Additionally, both incoming and outgoing planes are obliged to use the same runway direction.

If conditions allow, aircraft always take off and land into the wind. The reasons for this lie in the aircraft's aerodynamics. Lift is created more quickly on the wings under headwind conditions, which has the effect that the plane requires less distance to take off from the runway with all its wheels. Headwind is also favorable during landing, as it reduces touch-down speed and reduces the aircraft's braking distance. The length and width of the runways depends on the airport's usage purpose. Compared to smaller and lighter short and medium-range planes, heavy and large long-range aircraft require a longer runway due to their take-off mass. The aircraft's airspeed required for take-off and landing is calculated prior to every flight.

If the wind force exceeds the aircraft's permissible stress limits, patiently waiting for better wind conditions is often the only remaining option. Landing can be further postponed by *holding patterns* in the air and if the anticipated improvement in the weather does not materialize, pilots have to divert to the closest alternative airport.

What is an air pocket?

The term »air pocket« only exists in colloquial language and is rather misleading. Just like oceans, lakes and rivers do not have »water pockets« in the middle of them, the air does not actually have holes in it. Even if we cannot see air, it reliably surrounds us at all times and at all altitudes.

Nevertheless, it can feel as if the aircraft has fallen into a type of hole when it abruptly drops during a turbulent flight. There are several reasons for these sudden changes in altitude.

Airstreams can manifest as updraft or downdraft. These vertical movements make the aircraft drop or rise suddenly. Horizontal currents such as side, head and tail winds can also cause a bumpy flight. Some of these effects can be balanced or alleviated by means of the aircraft's rudders. The manufacturers specify a maximum speed for each type of aircraft for flying through turbulence. If they become more severe, the plane's cruising speed is adjusted accordingly. However, the differences are so minute that they cannot be felt. Only the engines become a little bit quieter for a moment.

Generally, weather changes and various air currents along the flight route are part of the flight routine, representing normal, if occasionally unpleasant, occurrences, as the air is constantly moving. However, neither *the aircraft itself* nor *you as a passenger* are in danger.

Planes and lightning

Commercial and private aircraft are struck by lightning several times during their service life. When compared to the countless number of flights per year, however, it is still an exceedingly rare occurrence. The chance of witnessing this during a flight are correspondingly low. How does lightning occur anyway?

Thunder clouds contain water droplets and ice crystals that rub together in the wind, creating high electric charges. The lighter ice crystals in the upper part of the clouds are positively and the heavier water droplets negatively charged. Once the difference in charge between the two poles is high enough, the energy is released via a lightning bolt. Airborne conductive particles such as dust and pollutants facilitate these electric discharges. Strongly heated by the lightning bolt, the air expands rapidly and breaks the sound barrier, which manifests as audible thunder.

Lightning and thunder are created at the same time. Since light travels much faster than sound, however, we perceive the lightning first. This effect also allows us to estimate our approximate distance from the thunderstorm. Every second that passes between the two phenomena accounts for roughly 1,100 feet (330 meters), meaning that if you can hear the thunder ten seconds after you have seen the lightning, you are two miles or three kilometers away from the thunderstorm.

Due to their metal construction, cars and aircraft make excellent lightning conductors. Aircraft fuselages form a fully enclosed casing, a so-called »Faraday Cage« that acts like a shield against electric charges. If lightning strikes the outer hull, it is routed around the aircraft and exits at a different point on its surface. Only protruding parts such as antennas or lamps attached to the fuselage can get damaged. This, however, has no effect on the aircraft's airworthiness or the safety of its passengers. After being struck by lightning, planes are checked on the ground before being allowed to continue operating without restrictions. Pilots and technical experts examine the lightning bolt's precise entry point and test the condition of all components as a precaution. Only a short time afterwards, the aircraft can freely continue its journey.

Thunderstorms and aviation

Studies estimate that, on average, 1,000 thunderstorms occur across the planet every day. Only one percent of all thunderstorms are categorized as severe. Generally, they can occur anywhere, but tend to happen more often in warm regions, as well as coastal and mountainous areas.

The aviation industry has been accustomed to thunderstorms for a long time. Airlines are well-prepared for their various consequences, while weather services do an excellent job of supporting flight personnel in providing safe flights.

Even though pilots avoid flying through areas of adverse weather, they cannot always completely circumnavigate these routes. By looking at the images produced by the on-board weather radar, they decide how close to a thunderstorm they can fly safely. Colored water drops represented graphically on the flight route ahead allow them to assess how likely it is that a new storm will form.

On the radar, the area in which the thunderstorm is located is indicated in red. Depending on the thunderstorm's size and intensity, the edges are shown in yellow or green. In case of a major thunderstorm, the yellow and green areas on the screen are narrow and the red area is more pronounced. If the screen shows such an image, none of the areas are suitable to be flown through. In case of smaller and weaker thunderstorms, on the other hand, the yellow and green zones are significantly larger and pilots can consider flying through the green area without any risk.

Two or more thunderstorms close together result in heavy turbulence when the aircraft passes them. These impacts can be very unpleasant and cause anxiety among the passengers. Even though turbulence can often not be avoided altogether, you might draw peace of mind from the fact that they pass and that pilots would never fly into the dangerous areas of the eye of a storm.

Isolated thunder clouds that are often surrounded by clear weather zones can be circumnavigated much more easily, however. They move much more slowly and therefore need more time to shift location, allowing aircraft to literally fly away from the adverse weather.

Since even smaller thunderstorms present possible risks such as heavy rain and associated hydroplaning on the runway, hail, snow showers, freezing, poor visibility and gusts, every respective piece of weather information must be assessed before departure. A rule of thumb says that the higher up in the cloud lightning originates, the more severe its intensity and the greater the chance of a storm are. Ensuring a safe flight is always the number one priority and so, bad weather is often a cause for delays.

The truth about turbulence

Rapidly changing air movements are the main cause of concern and anxiety among passengers. If you are already familiar with these sudden vertical and horizontal changes to the aircraft's attitude, you know how queasy this turbulence can make you feel. How dangerous is turbulence in fact?

It is not easy to describe how turbulence feels. We all experience its severity differently and even crew members' reports vary. Nonetheless, turbulence can be classified as light, moderate and severe according to its intensity and manifestation.

Light turbulence makes the aircraft start to wobble, yet objects not fastened down remain in place. Moderate turbulence can cause objects not fastened down to slide and fall. In order to protect the cabin crew, moderate turbulence will result in on-board services being halted.

During severe turbulence, loose objects can start flying through the cabin. They also put the organ of equilibrium in the human body to the test, as passengers regularly experience nausea due to the constant up-and-down movements. Extreme changes in direction and altitude mostly happen when aircraft pass through an adverse weather area.

Such extreme turbulence is extremely rare, however, meaning that the vast majority of passengers will be spared this unpleasant experience. Airlines put a lot of effort into shielding their customers from such negative experiences. Flight routes are changed or take-off times postponed already in the planning phase. In rare cases, flights can be canceled altogether because nobody wants to put passenger wellbeing at risk.

Measures can also be taken during the flight itself: pilots fly around areas with severe turbulence, avoid certain altitudes and steer towards calmer skies by climbing or descending.

One of the most common causes of turbulence is the uneven warming of the earth's surface, also called thermal lift. In the process, the aircraft alternately passes through zones of updraft and downdraft. Associated with correspondingly high solar radiation, summer temperatures can make themselves felt in the form of jerky movements. This turbulence is harmless but for passengers it evokes an unpleasant rollercoaster ride.

So-called *clear air turbulence* (CAT), which occurs in connection with high altitude winds, is a bit trickier, as it can neither be seen with the naked eye nor detected by the weather radar. Clear air turbulence occurs within a wide area and at irregular spatial and temporal intervals. Since it cannot be foreseen, it cannot be avoided either. This turbulence is also the reason why airlines recommend that all passengers remain seated and buckled up for the entire duration of the flight, even after the fasten-your-seatbelt sign has been switched off.

Although turbulence is scary, you should not worry too much. Aircraft are capable of withstanding enormous forces, a feat that is thoroughly tested before they are put into operation. US manufacturer Boeing, for instance, has subjected the wings of its »B787« plane, also referred to as the »Dreamliner«, to 150 percent of the expected maximum loads with no damage being reported. The tips of the wings were bent upwards with a force that would never occur in real life. Neither aircraft crew nor passengers can expect to ever experience such a showdown between the plane and the forces of nature.

Flying at high altitude

Commercial aircraft are built to fly at high altitude. The higher they travel, the more efficient, cheaper and safer the flight will be. Higher altitudes allow distances to be covered more quickly and, in many cases, adverse weather areas to be overflown. State-of-the-art computer systems calculate the optimum cruising altitude prior to every flight, allowing the best possible flying altitude to be precisely determined in conjunction with current weather conditions.

The direction of high-altitude winds, or *jet streams*, is marked on weather charts and is easy to predict. Tail winds are a welcome opportunity to bring you to your destination more quickly, allowing flight times to be shortened with the help of nature, in some cases significantly, depending on the strength and duration of the tail wind. They also make it possible to save large amounts of fuel. Entering and exiting these jet streams are often associated with turbulence, however. For many airlines it is therefore customary for the crew to briefly inform the passengers about this via loudspeaker announcements.

How condensation trails are formed

Condensation trails are formed at temperatures below -40 degrees Fahrenheit (the same in Celsius) which is why they allow you to identify particularly high-flying aircraft. Containing vapor and tiny soot particles, the emitted hot engine exhaust mixes with the colder surrounding air. The cold air at this altitude, however, cannot absorb the vapor emitted by the engines as well as the air at lower altitude, causing the water droplets to freeze to ice crystals in seconds. From the ground and in the air, you are able to spot these crystals in the form of condensation trails in the sky.

How long these frozen clouds remain in the air depends on wind force and, more importantly, on air humidity. In dry air, the water droplets evaporate quickly, as the air is able to absorb additional humidity until it is saturated. In this case, these ice crystals only remain visible for a short time or not at all.

In humid air, on the other hand, these elongated artificial clouds in the sky can be observed for longer periods of time. The air behaves like a saturated bathroom sponge. Water that cannot be absorbed stays outside the sponge, resulting in the ice crystals being visible for a longer period.

Make your own personal cloud: On a cold winter day, you can produce smaller versions of condensation trails yourself by simply exhaling. Your warm breath produces a small cloud in the cold surrounding air. Aircraft condensation trails are created in exactly the same way.

Flight Attendants & Pilots

How to become a flight attendant

Considering the fact that most modern-day flight attendants are female, it is hard to believe that this job was dominated by men in its early days. In 1912, German Heinrich Kubis became the world's first ever flight attendant. It would take eighteen years for American Ellen Church to become the first female to make aviation history in 1930. Then aged 25, the nurse managed to land a job in aviation due to her burning desire to take to the skies. Her job was to support anxious passengers during the flight. Not long afterwards, female flight attendants were employed all around the globe to take care of passengers.

Generally speaking, every airline decides for itself what pre-requisites and qualifications their cabin crew need to have. Key requirements include a minimum age, a minimum height, a high-school diploma, any necessary work permits, foreign language skills and a valid passport. School reports, certificates and a driving license are also usually requested.

Professional behavior, good manners and a distinct service mentality are expected, as are a well-groomed appearance and a friendly manner. After all, flight attendants are considered the figureheads of an airline based on their appearance. Uniforms turn these employees into brand ambassadors. Those who would like to work in this industry should also be open to other cultures and be able to deal with problems and disputes with a solution-oriented attitude.

Usually, the first step in the application process is to complete an (online) application form. Together with the applicant's resume and a photo, the airlines use the form to pre-select promising candidates. Companies often use telephone interviews to gain a first impression. Applicants who pass this step are then invited to a multi-stage selection process, where they are tasked with passing a series of tests. The main focus of these is on communication skills, the ability to work as part of a team, friendliness and command of the English language.

Systematic questioning helps determine and assess how much the candidates know about their potential employer. Airlines look for people who have considered their future work routine and who come with a corresponding level of motivation and work ethic. With a bit of commitment, they can prepare for these tests and practice at least some parts of them in advance.

Having passed the selection process, they are assigned to the next available training course. Usually six to eight weeks long, the course appears rather short but is demanding and requires intense learning from the trainees. First, they need to study general aviation knowledge and airline operation processes. The training course content ranges from rights and duties on board to an introduction to aeronautical meteorology, a first-aid course, human performance capabilities, life-saving measures and knowledge of the transport of dangerous goods.
Other lessons include flight-related commands, good teamwork and behavior towards passengers. Trainees furthermore learn how to walk the thin line between patient politeness and assertiveness. It is vital to always maintain the upper hand if problems or disputes occur among passengers, which is why the training puts a special emphasis on conflict resolution and on mediating between different cultures.

On board, cabin crew supply passengers with snacks, warm meals and beverages, depending on the airline's service concept. These are tasks that aircraft passengers notice, yet the main focus of the training course is on safety-related topics.

Aircraft crew need to remain calm in all situations and be available to answer any questions. They ensure that passengers board and disembark in an orderly fashion, make sure that hand luggage is stowed safely and that all passengers are sitting in their designated seats. With loudspeaker announcements, they address the passengers in several languages to provide valuable information on the flight. Additionally, at the start of every flight they explain the location and function of emergency equipment.

If airlines intend them to work on aircraft of several types, flight attendants need to acquire respective knowledge on all of them. These training courses include conduct in the event of an emergency, evacuation options, swimming and how to extinguish fires. These exercises are repeated until the trainees can perform them faultlessly. Both during the course and towards the end of their training, they have to prove their level of knowledge in written and oral tests.

Since this job also requires a good state of physical health, an aeromedical fitness test is also part of the prerequisites. Once the physician gives the go-ahead, the candidates can begin their careers over the clouds.

A day in the life of a flight attendant

Working in an aircraft cabin is not your typical 9-to-5 job. Those opting for this career should have a wide range of skills or at least the willingness to acquire all the necessary prerequisites. The wish to take to the skies is often based on childhood dreams and yearning.

Other deciding factors that drive the wish to exercise this profession include a sense of freedom, self-fulfillment in a job that is highly regarded among the public and the possibility to travel.

However, if you are considering a career in this industry, you should carefully weigh the pros and cons before applying. After all, shift work and irregular working hours are not for everyone.

A high level of individual responsibility, a global work environment and discounts represent motivating factors. A variety of short, medium and long-haul routes offer lots of diversity and flight personnel benefit from the fact that they do not have to take their work back home. Cabin crew do not need to complete any tasks at home, as is customary in many other jobs.

In the public eye, the profession is often falsely viewed as being a type of permanent holiday, always traveling to the most beautiful destinations. In reality, however, there are relatively few opportunities to pursue tourist activities at the destinations. In addition, not every airline offers overnight stays in foreign countries or daytime stays in cities abroad. This depends on the route network and duty roster. And even if flight attendants have time off abroad, it is not necessarily in a desirable destination. After all, airlines also fly to regions you would not dream of choosing for a vacation and even if they do, the free time available there is usually much too short.

Apart from this, the job involves certain exertions that might not be immediately obvious. Hundreds of flight hours per year can result in serious health issues due to irregular work hours. Constant time zone shifts, especially on long-haul flights, take their toll and can severely disrupt a flight attendant's sleep cycle.

Repeated absences from family gatherings and activities with friends can put a permanent strain on these relations and the same is true for all other types of relationships. After all, personal plans have to be subordinated to work rosters which are usually issued monthly. If you are furthermore responsible for children, you are forced to rely on other people's help during your absence.

However, the positive aspect of the legal framework of employee protection deserves a special mention. It includes work and rest hours, with close attention paid to compliance.

The size of the cabin crew depends on the aircraft's seating capacity. The Aviation Act specifies one attendant for every fifty seats in its regulations. This means that a medium-haul aircraft with one hundred and eighty passengers on board has four crew working in the cabin. Of course, airlines are free to use additional personnel, for instance for training purposes.

Depending on the airline's size, attendants might work in a different team on every shift. This regular change of colleagues allows no room for individual work methods. All work steps are trained until they are performed automatically, regardless of whether the team members have worked together before or whether it is their first shared flight.

If you would like to work with people in an international environment, enjoy interacting with people and are unfazed by living out of a suitcase, you can expect unforgettable impressions and varied working hours over the clouds.

Prerequisites for becoming a pilot

The image of the brave, ingenious and daring pilot has persisted for decades. And it is scarcely surprising, considering that they had little technical support to rely on in the early days of aviation. Aircraft were difficult to control and for a long time cockpits did not contain anywhere near as many automated systems as there are today.

Back then, people would risk their necks to make their dreams of flying a reality and consequently the job of a pilot enjoyed a high degree of respect and appreciation. Even though some attributes and clichés have stood the test of time, the public perception of the occupation is a different one today – not least because more and more women pursue careers as pilots. It is a regular job that can be learned like any other.

All those who want to fly high can make their dream come true as early as 18, which is the minimum age for obtaining a professional pilot license. If you are interested in training as a commercial or airline pilot, you need sound skills in the fields of mathematics and physics, a good understanding of technology and broad general knowledge. Moreover, your spatial visualization ability should be at the top of its game, as aircraft are navigated in the air in a three-dimensional space. Since English is the lingua franca of aviation, proficiency in this language is another must. Specific school diplomas are not required by law but may nevertheless be requested by the respective airline. Furthermore, a career in aviation requires a good physical and mental constitution and your medical fitness will be checked during the course of an aeromedical exam.

While some airlines train their own future personnel, others outsource this to various training organizations. Those who do not mind the financial risk can pursue training at a private flying school. High-quality training organizations offer comprehensive information and consultation to those interested. During these discussions, advice is given on the opportunities and risks involved in this career as well as answers to questions on financing options and the career outlook after successful graduation. In some cases, suitability tests are used to make you aware of possible learning difficulties early on.

Being directly accepted onto the training program of an airline, on the other hand, requires you to pass a complex admission process which is often divided into several stages and typically takes a few days. The exams are generally regarded as tough to pass, one of the reasons being that some aspects are tested under time pressure. This can include reaction tests and testing of your short and long-term memory.

Evidently, not every personality suits every company. This is why companies go to such lengths to get to know you and your personality and the reason why you and your fellow applicants are so closely screened in the form of group and one-on-one interviews. Most airlines furthermore request a psychological assessment with a special focus on your fitness to fly. Once you have passed all stages of the screening process, your complex training program begins.

Training as a professional pilot

To obtain a flight crew license, you need to prove your practical and theoretical skills. Aspiring pilots attend classes for comprehensive instruction about meteorology, principles of flight, instrumentation, electrics, navigation, operational procedures, mass and balance, air law and other focal points of aviation. Additionally, they are expected to self-study large amounts of content which is tested towards the end of every theoretical unit at the respective aviation authority.

Over the course of your training, you will learn your skills in airmanship on a number of different types of aircraft. Prior to every flight, you will be required to check the perfect condition of the plane and the faultless functionality of all measuring and flight instruments, as well as to quickly examine the landing gear and brakes. The first flight hours take place on single-engine training aircraft. During so-called visual flight, you need an unobstructed view around you and are therefore not allowed to fly into clouds.

Your first few training units will focus on the correct use of control elements and safe take-off and landing exercises that, naturally, also need to be perfected in difficult wind conditions. Only later will you learn how to use automated systems such as the autopilot.

After learning how to handle single- and multi-engine aircraft using their instruments, the focus will shift to »leadership« towards the end of your basic training. Flights with passengers always involve two pilots and often additional crew members are present on long-haul flights. So-called »MCC training« (*multi crew cooperation*) is designed to familiarize you with working in two-man cockpits. This involves professional teamwork in which every person knows their tasks and can implement them reliably and with careful accuracy.

After all, you may be required to make split-second decisions in the event of danger and unforeseen faults. Difficult flight maneuvers are trained in a targeted manner on flight simulators to make sure you can handle all possible situations confidently. This not only requires technical skills but also a high degree of emotional resilience.

Several factors determine the length of your training, as training courses can differ in procedure, duration, place and even the final pilot's license. There is often the choice between full-time and extra-occupational flight training. Just like every other form of training, much depends on your individual dedication and the training elements on offer. Although training standards differ from country to country, the content of civil aviation training is similar. After completion, nothing stands in your way of becoming a pilot on short, medium and long-haul passenger or cargo aircraft.

To reach this professional goal you will need, among others, a strong will, a high degree of personal responsibility, the ability to self-assess and a high level of enjoyment, without which you would not be able to complete the difficult training. Flying remains an absolute dream job for most pilots even with many years of experience.

Aircraft type training

Completion of the basic training to become a professional airline pilot is followed by mandatory *type rating* courses on the respective type of aircraft. In these further training courses you usually specialize in a manufacturer (e.g., Airbus, Boeing, Bombardier, Embraer, Tupolev, etc.) and typically, in a certain type or type family (e.g., Airbus-320-family and the types A318/319/320/321 or the Boeing B737 series etc.).

Type rating courses take on average eight weeks, depending on the airline's training package. During this time, the cockpit crew receives tough and intensive training, an important part of which is made up of many hours on full flight simulators that resemble the respective aircraft's cockpit in every detail. These training devices allow aspiring pilots to perform practical flight exercises and efficiently learn how to deal with possible system failures without incurring any risks.

The theoretical part of the training focuses on knowledge of all systems, the aircraft's technical performance and its proper use. At the end of it all, you will be required to pass a theoretical and practical exam covering all areas. Before your pilot's license is issued you will have to go through landing training with a real aircraft, albeit without passengers on board.

In addition, pilots return to the full flight simulator every six months. These recurring exercises are required to maintain the authorization to fly the respective aircraft type. The proficiency is evaluated in a test conducted by an authorized flight examiner, during which compliance with specified operational standards is also monitored.

Who flies the plane? Captain or co-pilot?

Functioning teamwork is a top priority in the cockpits of modern commercial aircraft, which is why it is set out beforehand who does what at every stage of the flight. While one of the two pilots is flying the plane, the other one might be monitoring the instruments or taking care of radio communication with the respective air traffic controller.

After every flight, controls are handed over to the other pilot, which means that you are alternately brought to your destination by the captain (commander) or the first officer (co-pilot). Both are fully-qualified pilots and are able to fly the aircraft alone in the event of an emergency.

The difference between the pilots lies in their responsibilities, determined by their respective ranks. The captain usually has more flight experience and makes the final decisions on board. These additional rights entitle the captain to request measures that may be required to ensure the safety of all passengers, crew, cargo and the aircraft itself.

Regardless of rank, further training and career development is available to both the captain and the first officer. Whoever meets the requirements can obtain a flight instructor license and, later, a flight examiner authorization.

Working as a check pilot, who is responsible for compliance with internal training and quality standards, is another possible career path. Roles in flight operation management, such as flight operation or fleet management, or as a technical or safety pilot, are also available.

Challenging airports

Generally speaking, every national and international commercial airport can be approached unless contrary provisions prevent it, as is the case with private or military airports, for instance. The aviation authorities categorize airports based on several factors. Not every airport is suitable for night flights or allows continuous 24-hour operation.

Airports are furthermore divided into degrees of difficulty based on geographical conditions. In many cases, mountains or nature preservation areas require deviating approach or take-off procedures. Some of these places require special flight simulator training before you are allowed to approach, for example Sion in Switzerland, Innsbruck in Austria, Kathmandu in Nepal, Seletar in Singapore or Aspen in the USA.

Sometimes local weather or noise protection measures lead to flight operation restrictions. For instance, only aircraft types capable of significantly steeper approach angles are allowed to land at London's City Airport, to ease the burden of noise pollution on the people living in the city center.

When it comes to airports and major hubs that are particularly difficult to approach, the airlines' training departments ensure that their pilots are properly trained in advance. During the flight itself, the preparations for landing do not differ, however, because no matter which destination the cockpit crew always have approach and departure charts at their disposal that ensure accurate navigation.

Safety & Wellbeing

How safe is flying?

The number of flight movements increases nearly every year and record numbers of passengers are reported on a regular basis. Aircraft are the safest means of mass transport and still, many travelers are anxious about setting foot in one. This is understandable, as many stress and fear factors come together during a flight. Most of them, however, are based on false assumptions, as well as lack of or misleading information. If you want to get rid of your concerns you should deal with them in detail. Comprehensive knowledge helps you obtain a better understanding of modern aviation safety.

Reports of airline disasters and incidents evoke different feelings to road accidents, even though both can be on a devastating scale. The likelihood that you know someone who will be killed on the road is many times higher than the possibility that you know someone whose life will be lost in a plane crash. In light of this fact, it seems paradoxical that people who possess a driver's license are afraid of flying. However, driving is much more familiar than flying as we partake in road traffic every day, even if as a pedestrian or bus passenger. We know the rules and therefore have a say. The thought of being able to stop at any time and to (seemingly) be in control gives us a sense of security.

These conditions do not apply to flying and most likely you also do not possess sufficient technical background knowledge to develop a satisfactory sense of security. In addition, there is the feeling of losing control, knowing that you have just placed your life in the hands of two strangers sitting in the cockpit. All these personal fears can dampen the enjoyment of flying. And yet, a few facts might make you aware of how safe flying really is.

In 2005, for the first time in history, more than 2,000,000,000 (two billion) passengers were transported on planes, a number that was doubled in 2017. These four billion passengers were spread across some 42 million commercial flights within a year. Statistically, more than 7,500 people boarded an aircraft every minute of 2017. This means that roughly 500,000 passengers were in the air at any given time.

When comparing fatal accidents, there is a marked difference between airplane travel and road traffic. More than 1.35 million people lost their lives on the world's roads in 2017, representing 3,500 people every day and one person every 24 seconds. The number of people killed in air travel seems low in comparison. In 2017, a total of 50 people died as a result of plane crashes, which equals less than one person per week.

A popular saying in aviation goes: »The most dangerous part of flying is the car trip to the airport«. Once you have arrived safely, you have left the riskiest part of your journey behind.

Cosmic radiation

Our home planet is constantly bombarded with high-energy charged particles from space, whose intensity is directly influenced by the sun's activities. On their way through the earth's atmospheric layers, this cosmic radiation continuously loses strength. But even without boarding an airplane, there is simply no way to escape this background radiation. Not just at great altitude but also on the surface of the earth, we are constantly exposed to naturally occurring radiation. One unit of this radiation is measured in *sievert* (Sv) and usually indicated in *millisievert* (mSv).

The average background radiation on the ground in Central Europe is between 2.5 and 3.0 millisievert, while many factors determine how much natural radiation people are actually exposed to. Apart from the building materials our homes consist of and basic foodstuffs, job-related activities and our lifestyle also have an effect on this value.

Flight passengers are generally exposed to very small amounts of additional cosmic radiation. The exact degree depends on the cruising altitude, flight route and duration and constantly varying atmospheric base values. Lowering the cruising altitude (flight level) by only 2,000 feet (600 meters) already decreases radiation exposure.

Due to the earth's magnetic field, the shielding effect against cosmic radiation increases along the equator which means that the degree of radiation passengers are exposed to is much lower on flights in these regions. In turn, radiation exposure increases the closer one gets to the polar caps, since the shielding effect diminishes in these regions. You will therefore be exposed to less radiation when flying from the United Arab Emirates to Mauritius as opposed to flying from Japan to Canada.

On a long-haul flight from the USA to Europe, you will be exposed to about 0.05 millisievert of radiation. If you have booked a return flight, the total exposure is comparable to having one lung x-ray done by your physician. If you increase that to twenty transatlantic crossings within a span of twelve months, the dose is equivalent to the annual radioactivity a heavy smoker is exposed to due to their own cigarette consumption.

Flying rarely or occasionally is regarded as harmless to the human body. During a 3-hour short or medium-distance flight, you will on average be exposed to 0.02 millisievert of radiation. More than three hundred such flights per year would be required to equal the radiation load received during one single computer tomography in the chest area (approximately 6 millisievert).

People who fly a lot due to their jobs and flight crew, on the other hand, belong to a group that is exposed to cosmic radiation much more frequently than others. Their average additional radiation exposure is 5 millisievert per year. Regular long-haul flights along the polar routes account for a radiation exposure similar to that of medical, scientific and technical personnel working with radioactive materials.

An upper limit of 20 millisievert of additional radiation per year has been prescribed to protect flight personnel. It is, however, highly unlikely that crew members even come close to this value.

Too much cosmic radiation is harmful to the human body which is why its potential danger should not be downplayed. However, excessive fear is also not called for. Making people aware of how to deal with our planet's natural radiation is a much better solution. In moderation, we can all continue to enjoy air travel as usual.

In case of an unforeseen incident

Most passengers pay no attention to them or even regard them as a nuisance. We are talking about the safety videos and safety demonstrations by the cabin crew prior to take-off. However, it could save your life to pay attention and listen closely to these brief instructions. In case of an unforeseen incident, the first few seconds are often crucial.

Once the fasten-seatbelt sign is switched off, many passengers open their seatbelts, even though it is advisable to remain buckled up for the entire duration of the flight, since turbulence can occur at any time. This does not mean that you have to forgo comfort, however. Keeping your seatbelt loose around your hips provides sufficient protection. On a calm flight, there is no reason not to go to the lavatory or stretch your legs in the aisle. And yet, more and more airlines are starting to require their passengers to leave their seatbelts on for liability reasons. This applies during the entire flight, regardless of whether the fasten-seatbelt sign has been switched off nor not. As a passenger, you then also share responsibility for not being injured in the event of turbulence.

In many evacuation exercises, aircraft manufacturers and airlines attempt to test various possible emergencies. The insights thus gathered not only have an influence on future safety instructions but also on aircraft manufacturing and the approval procedures for new types of aircraft. These exercises mostly take place on a so-called *mock-up*, which is nothing other than a demonstration model of an aircraft. It is used to simulate serious incidents such as an emergency landing on water or an evacuation on ground. Just like in a real emergency, passengers are asked to put on their life jackets, in case of darkness to follow the luminescent strips to the nearest emergency exit door, open it and evacuate the airplane model via the emergency slide.

These tests, however, repeatedly lead to the worrying result that only a small percentage of participants are able to properly implement the safety instructions. Surprisingly, frequent flyers fare no better than first-time or occasional passengers. The success of these exercises strongly depends on how much importance a person accords to the instructions at the beginning of the flight. Thus, the positive outcome of an emergency situation is directly linked to how much attention passengers pay to the safety demonstrations.

Airlines are well aware of this fact, which is why they generally attempt to convey the most important procedures in a compact and clearly comprehensible form, using carefully selected signal words. Some companies try to attract their passengers' interest with innovative videos.

Not all instructions coming through the loudspeakers are easy to understand, therefore leading to discontent. For example, you are asked during take-off and landing to put your seatback in an upright position and fold the table in front of you. Such on-board rules have an important purpose: in the event of an emergency, the small table can cause injuries to your abdominal area. In the event of an impending emergency landing, you are also requested to assume a *brace position*, in which you are asked to brace your body firmly between the rows of seats. You only have enough space to do so, however, if the person in front of you has previously put their seatback upright.

Seats in the rows closest to the emergency exits are popular among travelers as they offer more legroom than most other Economy Class seats, but not everyone is allowed to sit there. Cabin crew is instructed to make sure these seats are not occupied by someone who will themselves need support in an evacuation scenario. This includes children, pregnant women and all persons with limited mobility due to sickness or age.

When walking through the aisles, flight attendants will make sure that access to the emergency exits is unobstructed, no matter how inconvenient this might appear to you. Emergency exit rows must not be obstructed by hand luggage or jackets lying about. In the worst case, emergency exits might be the only way to evacuate the plane.

During take-off and landing, you are asked to keep the window blind open. In the event of an emergency, this gives you and the cabin crew unhindered views of the outside to get a clear picture of the situation. The cabin lights are turned off or dimmed during dusk and night flights for the same reason, making it easier for your eyes to adapt to the natural light conditions and find the luminescent strips leading to the emergency exits more quickly.

During their safety demonstrations, airlines inform their passengers that all carry-on luggage must remain on board in the event of an evacuation. In an actual emergency situation, trying to take hand luggage along with you would only waste precious time. You might even make it more difficult or, in the worst case, impossible for other passengers to get out of the plane. This is why you must leave personal belongings on board. After all, material goods can be replaced; human lives cannot.

Avoiding collisions

When it comes to accident prevention, the aviation industry is a clear step ahead of the automotive industry. While the development of collision warning systems for road vehicles is still in its infancy, this technology has been employed successfully in air traffic for years.

The so-called *Traffic Alert and Collision Avoidance System* (TCAS) is installed in every commercial aircraft and communicates with other planes in its vicinity. A screen in the cockpit shows all aircraft within a certain radius.

Should two planes come dangerously close to one another, the system triggers an alarm and the pilots can respond in time. They are shown a flight path that allows them to safely avoid the other plane. The TCAS specifies which plane is supposed to climb and which one is requested to descend. The systems are particularly helpful in areas with high traffic volumes and collisions are avoided reliably and effectively.

Safety or emergency landing?

Through the media, we often hear or read about emergency landings. This sounds very dramatic at first but on closer inspection, many of these »emergency landings« are in fact »safety landings«. If an incident occurs during a flight that does not represent an acute emergency (for instance a system fault warning), the cockpit crew immediately assesses the seriousness of the issue and evaluates possible risks. Since the safety of all people on board overrules the economic interests of the airline, the mere suspicion of a problem is enough to interrupt the flight and make an unscheduled landing. These are then referred to as safety landings.

In contrast, the term emergency landing refers to a flight interruption because of an actual, acute danger on board that makes it impossible to continue the flight. This can include serious technical defects, smoke in the cabin or cockpit, and especially medical emergencies.

Other aircraft and air traffic controllers are informed about the emergency with the distress call »Mayday, Mayday, Mayday«. The affected plane then receives immediate radio communication as well as approach and landing priority. If approaching the closest airport is impossible, the pilots' last resort is to land in an open field or on water.

When in doubt, go around!

The deliberate aborting of a landing maneuver is referred to as a go-around. This procedure can be initiated during approach if the conditions no longer allow the pilots to safely land the plane. In aviation, a go-around is not regarded as a dangerous situation, since it represents a prescribed procedure if a safe landing is impossible. Go-arounds are trained regularly and thus constitute a routine operation for cockpit crew.

The most common reasons for aborting a landing procedure include unfavorable weather conditions. Sometimes the surface wind force exceeds the plane's maximum load limits.
Insufficient visibility can be another reason, as the runway must be identified visually at a defined point during approach. If heavy rain or snowfall prevents this, pilots are required to perform a go-around maneuver.

Another reason concerns the scheduling of aircraft taking off and landing. To maintain traffic flow, air traffic controllers schedule aircraft of unequal speeds to lift off or land after one another. This scheduling is a daily challenge since, besides varying traffic loads, they must also take into account current weather data, the time of day, as well as preceding aircraft. Air traffic controllers are responsible for maintaining a minimum distance to every plane, which is not only important to avoid collisions but also because landing aircraft create wake turbulence that could hinder the following plane during its approach.

For many passengers, a go-around is an unpleasant experience. In an otherwise calm stage of the flight, the howling of engines suddenly increasing their speed can be startling, as they expect this to happen during take-off, not prior to landing. The pilots know that such a situation will make their passengers anxious and that they want to be informed about what is going on quickly.

However, the pilots must first concentrate on the flight maneuver to be performed. In fact, go-arounds are similar to regular take-offs. Only once they are done with this task can the cockpit crew inform the passengers about the reason for the go-around and about further intentions or proceedings.

If the go-around was prompted by adverse weather, holding patterns are considered. Once the weather improves, a second approach is initiated. The air traffic controllers once again include the plane in their schedules and accompany it on the radar until the final touchdown.

Rough or gentle landing?

Gentle, almost imperceptible touchdowns are favored by most passengers and usually receive praise and positive remarks. Rough landings, however, immediately receive criticism such as: »What a rough landing. They probably let the co-pilot land the thing«. Or: »That pilot can't have a lot of experience, judging by their rough landing«. Even supposedly funny statements can be heard: »We paid for one landing but got two«.

But how do pilots themselves assess their landings? You might be surprised to hear this but cockpit crew are only interested in one type of landing: a safe one. Whether it feels rough or gentle is secondary.

Safely landing an aircraft means touching down with the main landing gear first, followed by slowly easing the nose landing gear onto the asphalt. The wings are kept horizontal to prevent their tips from hitting the runway. Immediately after touching down, the pilots focus on the braking maneuver. At airports with a high traffic volume, they aim to leave the runway as quickly as possible to allow the next plane to take off or land.

The length of the runway also affects the braking maneuver, to make sure the plane comes to a stop in time even if the runway is short. Particularly short runways do not give pilots much time to get the wheels on the ground, which means rough landings are often intentional and necessary.

Moreover, certain situations such as adverse weather render gentle touchdowns downright dangerous. Standing water on the runway poses the real threat of hydroplaning. During a rough landing, the water is pushed aside by the landing gear, reducing this risk. The tires can quickly gain a grip and allow for a safe landing without losing control.

Applause after landing

Applause can convey a variety of emotions and be used in a range of situations. We clap to pay our respects to a particularly adept speaker, express our appreciation of an artist's performance or our approval during political debates.

It is less common to applaud tasks that are regarded as routine and unspectacular. And that is exactly the reason why applause after landing causes different reactions. While some think of the professions of pilot and flight attendant as just another job, others regard their work as impressive.

It is usually frequent flyers who are unimpressed by applause. They often use the plane as a means of transport and have therefore had time to get used to the procedures, sounds and emotions involved. Thus, they react to the clapping of less experienced passengers with varying degrees of understanding, embarrassment and even rejection.

While some find it completely over the top to applaud routine operations, others want to let the crew know how much they appreciate their performance or simply join in with the clapping.

In fact, however, that applause is usually not about the flight personnel at all, but more about the reassuring feeling of being back on the ground. And that not only applies to passengers suffering from fear of flying. Unfamiliar situations can make every plane passenger feel tense – a tension that is relieved at touchdown, which is then expressed with applause. After a turbulent flight, this feeling of relief also makes its way into Business Class and many a frequent flyer has been seen joining in with their fellow passengers.

But there are days when nothing seems to work out. Bad weather or technical difficulties can delay the flight. Cabin crew are aware of their passengers' concerns and annoyances and make every attempt to make the situation as pleasant as possible for them. Crews that go »above and beyond« with helpful or extraordinary services sometimes receive applause. But what do those who receive applause think about it?

Whether it be due to concerns, tension, relief or pure joy, flight crews are usually happy to receive applause. After all, nothing speaks against expressing appreciation; such a grateful attitude naturally flatters the crew. However, they by no means expect you to clap after landing. Their tasks are just too much of a routine for them.

Sometimes, pilots only learn later from their colleagues in the cabin that passengers clapped after touchdown. Depending on the type of aircraft, the sound of applause only reaches the cockpit faintly or not at all.

Regardless of one's opinion on this topic, it is obvious that this cordial sign of respect expressed by a happy passenger is a wonderful token of appreciation that will be gladly received by every crew member.

Dedication

I thank my lovely wife Bianca from the bottom of my heart for being so patient with me during the creation of this book. This work would not have been possible without her empathetic support and feedback. It is her foresight and her inspiring words that motivate me again and again.

My sincere thanks also go to my entire family and all my friends, whose support I can rely on at all times. Their helping hands and their valuable advice give me the opportunity to realize my goals and overcome new boundaries.

My appreciation also goes out to those people who have contributed directly or indirectly to the content of this book. Among them are all those who have asked me numerous flight-related questions throughout my professional life and who continue to keep me on my toes with their thirst for knowledge.

Thank you so much!

About the author

Mark Greenfield is a commercial pilot, entrepreneur and author. He discovered his passion for aviation in his childhood and adolescent years. As a pilot, he regularly flies to international destinations and looks back on many years of experience on many different types of aircraft, including exclusive private and business jets such as the »Bombardier Challenger 350« and passenger airliners such as the »Airbus 320 family«.

Over the course of his career in the aviation industry, he worked as a flight instructor for various training organizations, including six years in the management of one of Central Europe's biggest flight schools. As a member of an airline's selection committee, Mark Greenfield was also involved in the assessment of aspiring cockpit personnel.

In the framework of occupational counseling, the author also passes on his knowledge and passion of flying to future generations. Apart from his role as a check pilot, he still works as an instructor and speaker in the training of flight attendants, private and professional pilots as well as aspiring flight instructors.

Sources

www.security-label.de/baggage-tag/
www.aiaa.org/about/History-and-Heritage/History-Timeline
www.lilienthal-museum.de/olma/soest.htm
www.lilienthal-museum.de/olma/wright.htm

www.aerospace.honeywell.com/content/dam/aero/en-us/documents/
learn/products/recorders-and-transmitters/datasheet/N61-2083-000-
000_HCR-25-datasheet.pdf
www.atsb.gov.au/media/4793913/Black%20Box%20Flight%20Record-
ers%20Fact%20Sheet.pdf

www.timetableimages.com/ttimages/aerom.htm
https://en.wikipedia.org/wiki/In-flight_entertainment
www.imagikcorp.com/brief-history-flight-entertainment/
www.lufthansagroup.com/en/themes/flynet.html

www.boeing.com/news/frontiers/archive/2011/september/cover.pdf

www.airships.net/blog/worlds-first-flight-attendant/
www.worldhistory.us/american-history/ellen-church-the-first-flight-
attendant.php

www.iata.org/publications/pages/annual-review.aspx
www.iata.org/pressroom/facts_figures/fact_sheets/Documents/
fact-sheet-safety.pdf
www.icao.int/safety/iStars/Pages/Accident-Statistics.aspx
www.who.int/violence_injury_prevention/road_safety_status/2018
www.who.int/ith/mode_of_travel/tcd_aircraft/en/

www.bundestag.de/resource/blob/514148/81e5885cc3de
1721c0681d18c7636006/WD-8-018-17-pdf-data.pdf
www.bfs.de/DE/themen/ion/umwelt/luft-boden/flug/flug.html
https://odlinfo.bfs.de/DE/themen/was-ist-odl/strahlenbelastung-
vergleich.html
www.gov.uk/government/publications/ionising-radiation-dose-
comparisons/ionising-radiation-dose-comparisons

All sources last accessed on 26.03.2022